For t

by

'The Animal Psychic'

Jackie Weaver

Other books by the author:
Animal Insight
Animal Talking Tales
Celebrity Pet Talking
The Voice of Spirit Animals
Animal Communication from Heaven and Earth

Psychic
Book
Press.com

ISBN 978-1523723195

1ˢᵗ June 2016

To all the animals in this book, both on Earth and in Heaven, I am honoured to have been connected to you through my work and know of the love and happiness that you have brought into your owners' lives, and still do.

Darling Stan
2010 - 2013

My Darling Angel boy who is still looking down over me and helping guide me too. My heart still aches for him but I know he is never far away and always in my heart.

Introduction	7
Paul and his dog Tess	9
Shona and her dog Lexi	15
Mary and her dog Ollie	22
Katie and her rabbit Simon	26
Lisa and her horse Leo	31
Kathy & Mark and their dog Bonzo	37
Clwyd and his cat Topsi	47
Ian and his dog Jess	53
Susan and her dog Coco	55
Michael & Pearl and their cat Oliver	61
Letting Go	66
A Cruel Departure	68
Finding the Key	71
Coming and Going	75
In the Bank	79
Claire & Pete and their cat Chip	88

Diane and her dog Jess   92

Arwel and his dog Skye   99

Diane and her Song Thrush Flo   102

Kirsty and her horse Cuddles   111

Linda and her dog Saffi   117

Mark and his rabbit Bailey   124

Nichola and her dog Shakira   128

Beth and her dog Barnaby   133

Tracy and her Dog Hogan   138

Postscript   145

Introduction

If you have read any of my other books, you will be pretty familiar with my life story and the work that I do. I am not going to bore you with that, instead, I will summarise it for you...

I have always been into animals: brought up on a farm, vet nursed, taught people to horse ride and the list goes on. I really am an animal person and I keep my psychic work for them too. I have lost count of how many times I have been asked if I do 'people'. I often say, I should wear a t-shirt that says, 'I don't do people!' as animals need a voice and most of us humans can speak out-loud for ourselves.

In 2005 my life was to change forever... Having been so close to deaths door of Lymphoma, stage 4 (that means worse case scenario as spread throughout my body) but I survived and my survival seems to have been an inspiration to many too. This totally awakened my spiritual side and I do believe we 'come in with a date to go out' and it was obviously not my time.

In 2007 I gained the most wonderful friend Beth, who, as an animal psychic, came to read my animals and told me (through my dog, Sally) that I could do this too! She, like me, teaches (and keeps it very straight forward and simple) and true enough, I found, like many people, I could truly communicate with animals. These were not just animals living here on Earth, but with ones that are in spirit too. How my life was to change...

Although this is a serious subject, anyone that knows me, knows that I do like to have fun, and animals seem to relate to that and have a laugh with me too. I have been so very lucky as the media have picked up on what I do and apart from many newspaper / magazines articles, I have now reached mainstream TV too. I spend my time trying to let people know that animal communication is real and have been on: ITV *This Morning, The Paul O'Grady Show, Russell Howards Good News* and even *TOWIE!* I have had such fun and I know that I have reached people that needed help, and some who simply wanted to know what their animal had to say.

This is book number six and, for my first three books, I actually wrote the case stories on behalf of my clients. Due to work commitments I was struggling to do anymore but then found owners were more than happy to write their own stories of their communications for me to share with you. I still have quite a few stories written up by me, so I will include a few in here for you too. They have titles that I always try to do that allude to the story but don't give it away. I hope you enjoy this selection of genuine living and spirit animal communication stories.

A girl has her fame at last...

Paul and his dog Tess

Tess or 'Tessie Best Girl', as I liked to call her, was a black and white Dalmatian. She was in no way 'Dotty' when it came to intelligence; she was the most intelligent dog I've ever known. She had a personality and brain that was larger than life and sadly a belly to match; she did like her food!

Tess was born on the 8th July 2002 as 'Kins Mill to Kiss Chase' to a famous mum, a puppy that starred in the Disney film, 102 Dalmatians. As her name suggests, she was a pedigree through and through. She was a lady of stature, presence and etiquette. A lady that demanded respect. Under no circumstances would she allow dogs to kiss and chase her, everything was on her terms!

Fate brought us together in September 2002 when I discovered her advertised as the last puppy in a litter of thirteen. Someone was due to view her the day before but had gone to the address in Rainham in Kent, rather than Rainham in Essex, so fortunately for me geography had played a huge part in my 13 years of happiness.

It would appear that potential buyers, recognising her as the runt of the litter, had overlooked Tess; she was shorter than most female Dalmatians. Needless to say, her deficiency was more than compensated by her almost human nature.

Tess was very loyal and loving to her human family, and very maternal to those animals that crossed her path. In her younger years she would get in the rabbits pen to keep them company. Her maternal instincts inspired me to breed her, but unfortunately this was short lived as the two male Dalmatians chosen were either too much of a gentleman or too much of a headstrong youth! Fate had struck yet again, as her failed breeding programme had inspired me to introduce her to a twelve-week-old liver spotted Dalmatian called Molly in 2008. This is when her maternal instincts blossomed.

Tess doted on Molly and vice versa, but Tess played the Victorian matriarch role as both carer and authoritarian. Tess, like the rest of the family, saw Molly as the soppy and less intelligent girl, despite her now being seven years old. Perhaps it was because she was born on April fool's Day!

Tess would wash Molly's ears continuously, but bark or growl at her if she scratched the floor to crave attention or jump up at invited guests. Poor Molly was always under her thumb, but they loved each other dearly. Tess was a protector at all levels. Whilst she was not vicious at all she refused to let other dogs, or humans, come too close if they posed a strange sort of presence.

Tess was a lady of few barks and only barked when the need arose. She would greet people with a howl or almost yodel on the command of, "Say hello nicely!" This came in very handy when teenagers mimicked her bark or taunted her. As soon as I said, "Say hello nicely" the yodel would follow and they would run for the hills! Whilst barking wasn't her strong point, her whining was! She would whine intensively for food, particularly her chicken and rice or sausages, which she adored, or when she let us know that it was time for her to go to bed upstairs!

Her manipulation and craving attention could best be described as a child suffering the terrible twos! She manipulated us all to the bitter end, even enticing her to the garden to be clean was rewarded with a gravy bone biscuit! Despite that, her loving personality and her sad brown eyes could do nothing other than make her human family obey her every wish!

Throughout her entire life Tess remained strong, courageous and undefeated. Nothing fazed her or got her down. She suffered a severe injury, with the loss of her toe in 2008 during a dog attack, and then battled against leukaemia following diagnosis in September 2013. She had a series of operations to remove growths from across her body and attended weekly vet visits to undergo chemotherapy treatment. The vets were fascinated that she knew what stairs to go down and what kennel to go into, even without ever being told! Tess knew the drill and just got on with her life.

During her healthy years she would go to the park on a daily basis with Molly to play ball or fetch a stick, until the rain came! She hated the rain, but loved the snow! She decided what she wanted to do and I obeyed!

Every year she would love to go in the car to the coast where I have a holiday home. She loved the car. It was fascinating to see Tess and Molly running along the sand and in and out of the sea. Tess loved water but hated the rain. She clearly did not connect the two, even though she was highly intelligent!

There is no doubt about it, her life was luxury. She had the home comforts that every spotty girl deserves, even down to sleeping in her own dog bed and being covered up at night with her own cover!

It was only her last week of life that turned sour. From the 6th November 2015 her condition sadly deteriorated. She was no longer able to stand or walk unassisted and frequently had 'accidents', which had never happened. She was a clean lady and a lady with pride. The real turning point came when she refused to eat her chicken and rice and that was the point when I knew that sadly it was game over. Friday the 13th November 2015 is the day that changed my life. The vet attended her home at 14:00 hours and with all her family standing close by, (including Molly and the cats!) she turned to me to give me my last kiss and at 14:26 hours Tess slipped away peacefully.

In order to gain comfort from this loss I approached Jackie Weaver for a reading. I needed to know whether we had selected the right day for Tess to pass over to Rainbow Bridge, and to be assured that we had not let Tess suffer unnecessarily.

The evening before the reading was surreal, the once laid back Molly changed into an uncontrollable menace. She would not listen or go to sleep, but instead chose to scratch, pace and sniff the floor where Tess had been laying during her last hours of life, until 8.15am the following morning to be precise. She was like a dog possessed! Had Tess returned and panicked Molly? Who knows?

At 8pm on 30th November 2015 Jackie telephoned me. As soon as she spoke I knew that she had found Tess! Tess made herself known immediately by acknowledging her best buddy, Molly as a 'soppy unintelligent girl'. Poor Molly! Tess described their time spent by the coast and even acknowledged that there was a sea breeze where she is now, she did love being by the coast. She was also keen to let me know that that she also knew that Molly was now seven years old!

Tess observed her life as complete luxury and pleasure until the last weeks of life. She remembered having her own bed upstairs by the side of the family bed and having her own cover. She remembered her wrapped Christmas presents (which they were!) and her toys that had appeared beneath the settee in recent days! She was also very keen to point out that she was missing her food. No surprises there!

She acknowledged the years that she spent by my father's bed, particularly during his bout of cancer, and even called out his name, 'David,' to offer some validation to the somewhat cynic! She said that she had been there for him and that he had been there for her. She explained that she would greet my father in Heaven when his time finally arrives.

Tess remembered us all putting pressure on her belly to lift her up during her last week of life, but she understood that we were only doing our best for her. She felt the pressure around her neck and described the condition like 'lymphoma', which is true, as this is where her cancer was clearly visible. She also recognised that her life would be compromised by her condition and accepted that this was inevitable. Whilst Molly had realised this and was no longer moping, Tess asked her family to now do the same.

Tess remembered sharing her home with Molly and a number of cats, and was keen to convey that 'cats think they are the boss', she was also quick to add that she would never chase them. Deep down I think that she was implying that it was Molly who did, which is true! What a snitch!

She asked for six photographs of her to be placed on our Christmas tree in a circular mounted frame to allow her to be on all sides. Little did I know that my sister was in the process of ordering 6 glass baubles with her photograph on them! Tess added that 'the tree would look marvellous!' I never ever said that Tess was modest, and it is clear that she is still dictating from the other side of life!

Whilst it was not clear whether Tess had met other family members in spirit, she was keen to introduce her rather well-spoken neighbour here on Earth, who had passed recently. In a rather posh dialect the lady said 'shocking weather, shocking weather'. This lady obviously knew about the grim weather we're having here on Earth and I knew Tess had a soft spot for her. Tess truly hated the rain, so their conversation would have been so apt!

She remembered us all kissing her good bye before she slipped away, and was keen to point out that she was now with a rabbit and the still-born kittens that had gone before her. (Our cat had lost a litter many years before. How wonderful that they were in spirit too.) Clearly she had not lost her maternal instincts! She was still the loving and caring girl that she had always been here on Earth.

Tess thanked me for being a great Dad, and for us all shaping her into the well-behaved and respected lady that she was!

I have to say, the reading with Jackie opened up a whole new world and understanding for me. Whilst I have visited mediums and clairvoyants during my life, I had never really stopped to consider what happens to our beloved pets when they cross over, or even contemplated that they could communicate with us once they had gone. How wrong was I?

Jackie validated Tess and her life here on Earth and in Heaven. The reading provided complete comfort to both me, and my entire family, and provided complete understanding of what happens when the body fails us. The reading gave us all the reassurance that we craved, knowing that we had made the right decisions for Tess during her life and that her last couple of weeks had been full of love, not purely suffering.

The publishing of this story would not only allow Tess to live on in other people's hearts and minds, it would also allow her to leave this world famous, having been born to a famous spotty Mummy some 13 years ago!!

*****

One simply adorable little lady...

Shona and her dog Lexie

In 2002, as a family, we decided that we wanted to get a dog, and after researching the different breeds, we set our hearts on a West Highland White Terrier. In January 2003, we had to choose between two: a big bouncy boy, or a little female with runny eyes and a pink pot belly (from worms!) who looked like the runt of the litter. Of course we chose the little girl and we named her Lexie.

What a choice that was! She turned out to be the most loving and loyal companion that you could wish for, although she had health problems. It turned out that she came from a non-reputable dog breeder and for the first year of her life she was at the vets constantly. Amazingly, she didn't mind going, in fact, she simply loved being seen by the various vets!

Everywhere she went people would complement her and she would roll onto her back for them to rub her belly, she even accompanied my husband to work on one occasion. He was a fireman and even she wore a fire brigade armband as a coat! The firemen loved her and she lapped up all the attention.

She was a well-travelled dog – she went on her first long journey to Dorset at the age of only ten weeks old. She also visited Scotland on a few occasions, plus Devon and Norfolk. If I ever went abroad for a few days, she would stay with her beloved 'Nana'!

She had a coat for every occasion: a Santa Claus coat for Christmas, a cloak for Halloween, a dressing gown for after a bath, and so on. She always took the dressing up in her stride and was so adorable in her various outfits.

Lexie loved to play with her dog toys and loved you to chase her. Her toys mainly consisted of anything green (!) and hedgehogs! Although people say animals are colour blind, Lexie would always pick anything green out straight away; she literally preferred her green toys over anything. Every time Lexie went outside into the garden she would always run and fetch her favourite toy hedgehog. She would take it out with her and if she had left it outside, she would sit at the back door and grunt at you until you let her out to go and get it back in!

She loved any fuss and, although she very rarely barked, she used her paws all the time to get our attention. She would paw us to ask us to stroke her and would do anything for a biscuit, and would paw the cupboard door until she got one. She would help to empty the shopping bags, to see if she could smell anything in it for her; on occasions she had even been found having climbed right inside the shopping bags to check them out thoroughly.

When Lexie was four-years-old we got another Westie to keep her company, although I'm not sure how wise this was! Lexie liked to show her who was top dog, and if the younger dog, Polo, sat next to us, Lexie would stare at her until she got down. This used to make Polo very grumpy and often we would have to tell Polo off for growling, although we could understand why she was annoyed. We always say that Lexie is a little lady and we used to call her a princess and Little Lady Lexington! When Lexie developed her bad cough, she would often cough a lot and sometimes it would make her trump (pass wind) at the same time! (My daughter wanted me to include this as it used to make us giggle at her reaction.) This always shocked her, as she would wonder where that awful sound came from! We used to say she always looked embarrassed and that a lady would never do such a thing! It did always amuse us though! Sorry Lexie! We always joked that if Lexie was human, she would have been a lady that lunches and drinks champagne!

Lexie was a little lady of routine and liked things done her way! She liked to be in bed for 9pm and she was allowed to sleep upstairs on our bed. Bang on 9pm Lexie would sit at the door waiting to be let upstairs. She always had a biscuit before bed and, as the bed is quite high and Lexie was only little, she would turn her back for you to pick her up and put her on the bed ready for her biscuit and sleep! (Jackie actually mentioned about this to us in her reading.)

In 2014 when Lexie was eleven, we noticed that she was drinking a lot of water. We took her to the vets and, after tests; they informed us that she had a problem with her liver, possibly a tumour. I didn't want her to undergo any further invasive tests as, by this time in her life, Lexie had gone off vets! Also, she wouldn't have been well enough to withstand the treatments on offer for a cancerous tumour anyway. The vet gave us supplements for her liver and she carried on quite happily for a further year.

In February of 2015, she began coughing and bringing up fluid. She went back to the vets and he gave her bronchodilators (these help the inside of the lung dilate) which helped for a few weeks, but then she began to deteriorate again. We had a few bad nights and it was with a very heavy heart that we took her to the vets fully expecting that he would say she needed to go to sleep... that forever sleep. However, she had a reprieve that day, as he gave her some steroids which really picked her up, although we knew it would be short term. Their effect lasted for a few days and she made the most of that time. She ate like a horse and we gave her lots of biscuits and chicken for her dinner. We had some lovely days together and I will treasure that time.

Towards the end of the week she started to get worse again and I took her to the vets to see if he could give her anything else. He said there wasn't and that he would put her to sleep there and then if we wanted him to. I was unprepared for this and so took her home. For the last few nights we had been sleeping downstairs on the settee with her and that night I did the same. She had a terrible night. I nursed her and we had lots of cuddles and kisses together. I made an appointment for the vets for lunchtime the next day and she was put to sleep. She was so calm; it really was as if she knew what was happening. I was absolutely heartbroken and beside myself with grief.

My family and I are big believers in white feathers being sent to you by your Guardian Angel. These white feathers appear as a sign from a loved one who has passed away. They are often sent to you at a time of need or when you are thinking about someone who passed over. As my birthday had been approaching, my daughter ordered me a handmade white feather necklace. On the day that we had to say goodbye to Lexie, my daughter received a message to say that the white feather necklace was on its way to us. We both thought that this was very significant and that it was Lexie sending it to us, and it will always be a reminder of Lexie.

I began researching books on animal bereavement and came across Jackie. I contacted her to make an appointment for a reading and coincidentally, Jackie had been on TV on the *Paul O'Grady* show the very day that Lexie died.

Jackie rang me at the appointed time and explained what would happen during the reading that we would have a three-way-conversation with Lexie. Jackie said that she had asked Lexie to come forward and connect with us. She began by saying that Lexie liked attention and was all 'me, me, me' and, 'just me' although, saying that, as much as she liked attention, she never barked much. This was so right.

Jackie then said that Lexie was talking about being taken somewhere, like a workplace, where everyone said she was gorgeous. At first I couldn't place this, but Lexie was insistent and later on I remembered the fire station. (As soon as I clicked, I dropped Jackie an email to tell her!)

Jackie then astounded me by saying that Lexie had a cough and fluid around her heart and this really slowed her down. Jackie couldn't have known this from anyone else, as I hadn't given her any information. She also said that she had been ill for about six weeks, but that we had an extra week and that was a special time. (Over six weeks she had gone back and forth to the vets in desperation to try and help her.) Jackie also said that I had 'nursed her like a baby' and wrapped her up and held her close. She said that I used to say; "Give Mummy kisses" and that we had an amazing connection and Lexie said we were very lucky to have shared our lives together.

Jackie also said that she felt I was a little psychic myself and that I had thought I'd dreamt of Lexie after she died, that I heard her pawing and pitter-pattering on the floor. Oh my goodness, so it wasn't a dream! Jackie explained that it was a visitation from Lexie herself. Lexie said that I knew she was okay and said, "It's okay Mum, we had a lovely time."

Jackie knew about that piece of jewellery I mentioned earlier and the significance it held for me – Lexie said it was beautiful and, bearing in mind it arrived after she had passed, to know that she could see it, made it all the more special.

She also told Jackie that we used to dress her up and that I was thinking about getting a tattoo and that it wouldn't hurt! Jackie said she felt it would be more cartoon like than an actual picture, and so true – my daughter and I were discussing getting a little paw print tattoo. Jackie mentioned that we had a book with Lexie's picture on it. We had, as my daughter had just had a notebook delivered on the day of the reading and it had a picture of Lexie on the front!

There were other bits of information, such as my other dog just liked to be naughty for the sake of it! She also said she had skin problems and not to use chemicals on her – just baby shampoo. She even offered that my daughter had a problem with her eyes when she used eyeliner so Lexi said to be careful what she used! I didn't even know that, but my daughter confirmed it was true!

I was very distressed at having Lexie put to sleep so I asked Jackie if Lexie knew what was happening. She confirmed that she did – she had been privy to all the conversations and had taken it in her stride. She said that on the day I was physically quaking, and at this point Jackie made me laugh and said that Lexie was giving away my secrets, as I had gone home and had a good drink afterwards. I do confess to having a few brandies!!

Lexie said that I was stronger than I thought and that I had her picture next to her ashes, and, "There will never be another me." This is so true – she was a character, a real one off. I miss my beautiful girl like crazy, but at least now I am sure that we will be together again one day.

Thank you Jackie for assuring me that Lexie is safe and well in Heaven, just as we believed she was and is now just simply 'living elsewhere'. Sweet dreams my darling Angel.

*****

A sticky situation...

Mary and her dog Ollie

I had recently taken early retirement and together with my partner, we wanted a dog, as we were now in a position to care for one. We debated about this simply because I would not go abroad and leave my pet in kennels, so that was a sticking point. On Christmas Eve a close friend, who has a dog, came to visit us. I mentioned about an advert for a Yorkshire terrier and when I told her why I had resisted she said, "Don't be silly, I will look after it." So, with phone calls made, and a mad rush to a pet shop to get all we needed over the Christmas period, by 6pm Ollie, as we christened him, was ours. We were so delighted as we looked at him in his new bed safely tucked into a warm blanket.

Ollie is a jet black and rather large Yorkie. He is quite a character who knows his own mind and will not be persuaded... whatever! I loved showing him to everyone, but at the beginning he would not go for a walk. He point blankly refused to move, he just planted himself down and would not budge. No coaxing or persuasion would get him to walk and then one day he spotted my neighbours up ahead and we were off, and never looked back!

One evening, whilst at a friend's house, he gave a little whimper and refused to put his back paw on the floor. The next day I took him to the vets and it turned out there was a problem with one of his joints. The vet bandaged it up and I had to keep him on restricted movement for a couple of weeks. As much as we tried, this proved to be pretty impossible. After the two weeks (and a cancelled holiday) the vet said he needed an operation. I had to leave the vets without him and as much they tried to tell me he would be okay, but just leaving him there upset me so much. It felt like I was abandoning him in a place he didn't know and I would not be there to comfort him. To this day I like to have my partner with me if I am taking him to the vets.

He recovered quickly from his operation, but unfortunately his thick coat was matted and knotted where the sticky plaster had been applied. He also sported a bald patch where the operation scar was. I took him to the groomer who struggled to cut his hair and suggested I stayed next time. I did stay next time but we struggled to hold Ollie for her to cut his hair. Each time I took him, he got even more determined not to be handled. The vet gave me a pill to give to him to relax him, but that just exasperated the situation. I was at my wits end, as leaving him with a long coat just encouraged his coat to knot despite my extensive grooming each day.

Whilst looking at Amazon books I came across Jackie Weaver's free eBook. I read this and then bought her first book. By this time Ollie's coat was very long and thick. He had also started to get me up every night wanting to go outside for a wee; this was after his late walk so it didn't make sense. He was also acting very nervous and anxious with noise, in particular fireworks, which annoyingly are used for parties and all sorts of celebrations nowadays.

I decided to contact Jackie to see if she could help me and the reading was amazing. Jackie told me about him sitting next to me on the settee, which he always does, and various other things. I brought up about him not letting the groomer clip his coat etc. Jackie explained to me that Ollie would not let the groomer touch him as she hurt him. He said, 'It was hell!' He went on to say that the clippers made his skin raw and his feet were all over the place. I remembered the bath was slippery and there was a struggle. He said the fear made him feel sick and I said I had felt uncomfortable about it, but she was the professional so I had trusted her.

Jackie then asked if he had a problem with his leg. I explained that he had had fracture but he actually corrected me and said, "No... a contusion!" Jackie and I did not know what this meant so we looked it up on the Internet and found out it meant: 'a bruise, blow or bang without broken skin'. I then recalled that when he whimpered about the time he had attempted, without success, to jump up onto a chair – he may have knocked it then. He admitted that he got miserable as time went on with us restricting him and added that the sticky tape had been trapping his hair so was nipping him under his arm. This explained why he was very resistant in the vets when the dressing was changed which, unfortunately for him, was almost every other day. Normally he was so friendly and would let the vet handle him, but now seemed so anxious. He said he was not an anxious character but anxious of what had happened. I loved how he had corrected what was said.

Jackie tried to explain to Ollie that he needed to get his coat groomed and that the pulling hair was only because he had had a sticky dressing, which he no longer has. She also told him that if he didn't get groomed his hair could get knotted and then it would feel as sore again. His response to that was, "They can do my tail, it does not hurt!" There were offerings of words like 'brave boy' and 'so soft' that Jackie suggested I use as he had requested them.

Jackie did say that she could not promise he would change but hoped that he would maybe try, especially as he had offered about his tail. I eventually found another groomer, I explained to her that he may, or may not, let her touch him and I would bath him myself before taking him. (I thought that at least if he did not have to fear slipping in a washing area, then at least that would be a start and help his confidence.) She agreed to take him on a quiet day and not force him if he was resistant. She would start with his tail to show trust and see how he felt. I waited at a cafe next door, and when I collected him he was absolutely fine and she said he had been a good boy. I continue to bath him first and take him there and she says he relaxes and lets her clip him with no worries.

As for the night wetting, Jackie had suggested we tell Ollie to properly empty his bladder, (not just have a quick pee) before going to bed for the night. Amazingly it worked! He makes us laugh because every night at 10pm, regardless of anything, he gets up and walks to the door. He goes into the garden for a proper wee and then takes himself up to bed!

As you can see the reading really helped although, sadly, he is still petrified of fireworks, but as he said, "It hurts my ears." There is not much we can do to help him apart from turn the TV or music up if we are aware of them. One time, whilst on a lead, he heard something that sounded like a gun shot and yanked the lead out of my hand and ran off. In complete panic I ran home crying my eyes out, only to find him waiting for me at the gate having crossed two roads! Words cannot describe my relief. Jackie suggested I always tell him to come back to me if he is afraid. I still do this four years later, and so far he has always come back when I call him.

Thanks Jackie for helping us with our boy. All the things that came up in the reading truly gave us a real insight of his perception of life: his logic, sense of humour, stubbornness and how he could correct what we as humans say! Bless him.

*****

An Angel with lop ears...

Katie and her rabbit Simon

My daughter Emily wanted a bunny and chose him. I was very wary of bringing such a responsibility into the house and another mouth to feed. I had been made redundant three months ago and was worried about finding another job. I said we should sleep on it, and if he was still there tomorrow, we would have him, but only if I could call him Simon!

To be honest, I dearly hoped he had been bought by someone else, but the next day he was still there. Inside I was kind of disappointed, but when Emily gave me the big watery-eyed look I had to give in and get him. Getting him also entailed a very expensive hutch, which actually took two trips to get home in my two-seater sports car!

Incredibly I was instantly smitten – this beautiful white lop-eared bunny who ate through cables, wires, designer handbags, skirting board could do nothing wrong! "It is only 'stuff'" I would think and say! He'd play dead, bounce in the hall, follow me outside, and lie in the sun. I had hit a couple of years of grey, gloomy depression and my Simon saw me through it all. He would jump up on my bed and nudge my head for a love, he'd eat raisins out of my clenched teeth, and he would open doors and run to me. Every day I felt so blessed; he was such a beautiful boy. We even shared the same birthday, well, I kind of fabricated that, but he would have been born around the same date so that was good enough for me!

I then got a job miles away and had to work down South all week. It was time to get Simon a friend, and we did. Our lovely Karen arrived, they fell in love and were inseparable. It was touching to see them together and share their relationship. I eventually came back to work nearer home and got to spend more time with them both. Better still, I was about to start working at home which meant I could be with my pets all the time! Yes!

I had been putting off clipping Simon's claws for ages (it was one of his least favourite activities) but the scratchy sound of slipping bunnies on the floorboards was getting too much and I knew they needed doing. On Friday night I set about clipping them and somehow he frisked off my lap and hit his head. He wandered off as if nothing had happened but then I saw his eye was damaged. I rushed him to the emergency vet. They said it was not a major operation to fix it but sadly, he didn't wake up. I have never been so upset. I couldn't eat and I couldn't sleep, the bond with Simon was so strong – it was immense.

I knew I had to find a way of moving forward and finding comfort. I was seeing spiritual signs everywhere: wagons stuffed full of hay and straw overtaking me on the motorway; 'Si' tags on graffiti; our initials on number plates. Since becoming depressed once more, I really delved deep into my spiritual side, so decided to try and feel Simon's presence more. I had no idea that there were people who could communicate with animals, but something compelled me to research it and I found Jackie. I felt that she would be able to help me heal.

We set up a webcam call, which was a week after Simon had passed. I couldn't wait, but was dreading it in the same measure. Jackie opened our chat with Simon telling me that he had communicated with me already and that I have very vivid dreams – we spoke about this in more detail and it gave me the assurance that we had all connected. Simon then announced that he is a 'real-not-afraid-boy' and massive giggles from us ensued at his choice of descriptive words. I commented on his lack of eloquence, saying I thought he would talk better than that, but agreed that he definitely is not a timid bunny – not like Karen who is actually twice his size!

The remainder of conversation with him was wonderful. He mentioned the fact that we 'shared dinner' (the raisin thing!!) and that Mummy doesn't eat much (sadness!). He mentioned a stuffed toy that he thought looked like him! Jackie was not sure about what she could 'see', but I explained that I had been thinking of getting a lovely lady in the US to make a felt model of him! Jackie said Simon thought this was a 'marvellous idea', which was hilarious! Simon also told Jackie that my working hours are changing, which they were. I was about to start working from home all the time (as I had mentioned) and was so looking forward to bonding with him more. At this point I did nearly lose myself to tears.

Jackie gently asked him why he had passed over. He told her he'd had an incident, it felt weird, but he had no pain and then went to sleep. He reassured me that it was 'no blame'; she went on to say that it actually seemed as if he didn't even notice what had happened. This gives me relief when I think about it, because he didn't react, he did just wander across the room. He also 'sat on her lap' (mine!), wonderful. He told Jackie just how I used to kiss his head and stroke his lovely lop ears. He showed her how he would run to me, and also how he would use his head to open things and nudge with it.

At this point, he made me laugh as he fibbed; he distinctly blamed poor Karen for all the chewing that had been going on! He was 100% the culprit and I pointed out that there had been no chewing since he has gone! He was such a gem, but that is one thing I don't miss. He offered a picture of his Karen to Jackie who, bearing in mind had a picture of a stunning Simon bunny, cautiously described Karen as having 'odd bits of hair sticking out here and there.' I laughed and said yes she has, and that she has one ear up and ear one down – Karen is truly a one off bunny, definitely not a standard one!

Bringing the conversation back to him, and avoiding any more discussion on 'blame-shifting', he mimicked, "SSSSHHH, quiet it's night time." I laughed at my cheeky boy, but he was talking about my insistence that the nocturnal ones had to go to sleep when I did! He talked about sorting the yummy (fattening) bits out of the bunny food to eat, which is how he got his nice rounded tummy.

Jackie asked if I wanted to ask him anything, and I did. I had gone and got Karen a new playmate, pretty much straight away, and he was called Alasdair. Bless Simon; he then went on to say Alasdair was a 'cool dude'! I was pleased to hear his positive thoughts and explained to Jackie that he was. In fact, he had been a proper show rabbit and had many girlfriends. Then suddenly Jackie started to giggle and said, "Well, if you think of it from the animal's point of view... here we have 'Mr Show Bunny' and then he meets Karen, who does not conform to any show standards." Laughing she said, "Can you imagine his words on their first meeting? "Well hello, but I have never seen one that looks like you before!'" But, as they say, looks aren't everything; they seem very happy in each others company, which Simon was pleased about.

As we were about to finish, Jackie touched her own neck and said he was showing a necklace that looked like it had a bunny on it. I did have one, I had only just bought it on the eve of his death – perhaps a portentous message from the Angels, which I took as bad luck and wouldn't wear it. Simon asked me to put it back on and wear it with love from him.

Simon said he'd had a good life; he was not treated like a rabbit, and told me that my life was going to change positively! I feel this too, and understand that everything happens for a reason, but I would so love to have him back.

The chat has uplifted me so much I feel really connected with my boy again, so much that I am able to shower my other rabbits with lots of love without guilt. I was told things only Simon and I would know. It really has given my faith in spirituality such a fuel injection. I have retold the story to so many family and friends. Even my daughter, who is a huge cynic, was so moved by it she made me stop telling her everything that was said.

This has been a beautiful experience that has helped me through a very tough time and one that will never be forgotten.

*****

Her beautiful Peter Pan...

Lisa and her horse Leo

I have always had a passion for animals, but more precisely horses. As a child I was obsessed, but due to a lack of funds and other elements meant I couldn't have a pony. I watched as many videos as I could and whenever I had any pocket money saved, I would buy myself a riding lesson. Locally, there was a Welsh Cob breeder who was old fashioned (and in my opinion sometimes cruel in his training methods) but I started to ride his young horses for him. In those days, for me, the more crazy the horse the better; I loved the challenge and would ride anything! If there was a horse that he thought would not make it as a sensible riding horse, he would take them to the local horse sales. They would be sold whatever and often their future was uncertain. I bought my first horse, Charlie, from him who himself was destined for the sale ring. I still have him 19 years later!

Quite a few years later he asked me if I would come and ride his new stallion. He was a stunning Welsh cross Arab with an attitude to match. His first foal was a filly that I bought and called her Sianne. That same year my granddad passed away and left me some money, also my partner and I had just bought our first home together with land attached. Out of the blue, the breeder phoned me one day informing me that he had Sianne's full brother for sale. Apparently he was stunning and would be bigger in height than Sianne. Initially I said I wasn't looking for any more then, one day I drove past and just had to stop and see him. He was indeed stunning. That day I sat in the field for about an hour while he approached me and snuffled into my hair then strutted around the field and came back to me out of curiosity. I called the breeder and informed him I would have him. The name Leo came to me straight away. I realised what the connection was, as I was buying him out of the money left to me by my granddad and at his funeral, the song *When I Need You* by Leo Sayer was played. So Leo it was.

From the minute we brought him home he was a big character on the yard. He always made me laugh, snuffling in my hair and would gently nibble any ribbons or loose ropes. I will always describe Leo as being 'quirky'. The things I expected him to have a problem with: first dentist treatment, first set of shoes etc. didn't faze him, but the everyday simple things, like the hose being dragged across the yard, would cause him to freak out. I spent so much time with Leo that when it came to breaking him to ride, it was an easy task and he took it in his stride. Once he was broken and working well with me, I asked a good friend of mine to have a try on him but, bizarrely, he wouldn't let her even put her foot in the stirrup without shooting off. At this point I realised the trust and bond that we had and he was definitely 'my boy'. Over the next few years I had two children and on three occasions I tried to loan Leo out. The longest he lasted was six days! These were all friends who knew him but couldn't do anything with him off my yard. When I went with the trailer to collect him, I could almost hear him say, "I told you I would be back!"

While I was pregnant in order to keep him working (no one else would get on him!) I bought a blow up doll from the Internet and tied it to the saddle! Anyone passing must have thought I had lost the plot but it worked and he was happy!

Although Leo was lots of fun, he was also on occasions unpredictable and stubborn. Loading him in the trailer could go two ways; he would either walk straight in, or fight with me. He was very strong but I wouldn't give up. Although I felt that I 'got him' he also caused me many injuries: black eye, split lip, broken thumb, but I was determined not to give up.

When Leo was almost eight-years-old I decided I needed to get him riding properly and achieving my goals together. I started working him more consistently and discovered he had an amazing jump. One day, while riding in the school, he almost sat down and ducked out from under me. I fell flat on my backside and was completely confused as to what had just happened. This occurred again, so I had his tack checked and his back treated but was then advised to keep riding him. This was a new behaviour for him, as I had seen him buck when other people rode him, but he was always well behaved for me. Over the years I was told time and time again to just sell him, that he was dangerous and to get rid of him. I wouldn't give up on him, even when hospitalised with a suspected broken neck! During one lesson I fell off twice which resulted in a broken coccyx. This was the last time I ever rode Leo and I felt at my lowest ever with him – how could this horse be so good then, all of a sudden, do what he did for no apparent reason? Very briefly I contemplated selling him, as I felt I had done all that I could do with him, and maybe that would be the best option for us both. My friends said his show name should be Leo Casino as it was Russian roulette whether I would stay on him or not! However, in my heart, I really felt there was more to it than just 'bad behaviour'.

It was at this point that I first called Jackie to communicate with Leo, as all the checks I had done didn't give me any answers. Leo explained to her that he couldn't control his sudden explosions; it was like a sudden nerve pain going through his body. This all made perfect sense to me, as when he was about to spasm I could feel him hold his breath; it was something that he had no control over. He said he did trust me and asked for my forgiveness. During this communication he described himself as being 'Mummy's boy' which is what I had called him all his life. Jackie said that she really felt that his behaviour was from discomfort and at least he had been able to give his side of the story. I agreed. He said he had had treatment that had helped a bit but had never been properly investigated. This was true as he had never been to the vets for X-rays or scanning. He also told me that he wouldn't kick my dog! True – he never did.

Following the communication, I decided to give him time off. He had a fantastic summer out at leisure with his field companions but at the start of the winter I noticed his behaviour change. He would distance himself from the other horses and would be standing alone. One day I went into the field and the gate was all bent. I stood there for a few minutes in bewilderment scratching my head as I didn't know how the gate had become so bent. I remember loudly asking, "Has anybody got anything they want to tell me?" but passed it off as one of those things that happens when you keep horses. Leo's behaviour became more unpredictable and he would 'shoot off' when being led in and was unable to hold his leg up for the farrier to trim his feet. I knew that I had to get the vets involved, as things were really adding up to physical problems causing these issues that were now exhibiting on the ground, and not just from a riding point of view.

Leo went for back X-rays and I had anticipated a call saying he had kissing spine (this is where the bones can touch) and it would be fixable. However, I was shocked when the call came to say his spine was actually deformed and probably couldn't be corrected. They expressed that the likelihood would be that he would become more dangerous and I should maybe consider putting him to sleep. They did however say they did not think he was in any pain, just reacting when it occurred. When I went to pick him up, they asked me if I would prefer to leave him there and it (putting him to sleep) would all be done without me. This was not an option for me. Leo was ten and had lived his whole life at my yard so I felt I owed it to him for his passing to be at home too. In my head I had made my decision based on his behaviour, and my gut feeling was that he should not have to suffer these pain episodes and things were likely to get worse. Even the sweet little things he once did had changed which spoke volumes to me. My heart was not as easy to convince, so again I contacted Jackie for a conversation with him about my decision.

One of the first things Leo said was, "I am fine with it." He thanked me for giving him a way out. He explained that when I watch him going around in circles in the field it was because he was trying to relieve the pain and he was struggling with it now.

He gave me five reasons why it would be the right decision and what touched my heart was that he was saying he recognised he is unsafe around me, my children and the other horses.

In relation to the gate that I mentioned earlier, Leo wanted to let me know that he did it when he had a spasm and kicked out! Although quite serious, this made me laugh as he must have heard me asking that day if anyone had anything to tell me.

This communication convinced my heart that having him put to sleep would be for the best for him. He said he wanted to be remembered by me as 'Peter Pan' because he never grew old, which is such an accurate description. He was so convinced that it was what had to happen, that he even suggested a day later that week for it to happen!

Leo died on 27th January at home. Although it remains the hardest decision I have made, I know with absolute certainty, thanks to Jackie's communication, that it was the right choice to make and has made the grieving process easier to embrace. Now I will always remember Leo as my little Peter Pan (as he so sweetly suggested) and all those moments that I was cross with him I know have been understood and forgiven. I know Leo was meant to come into my life and live his life out with me and that I owed it to him to help release him from his body that was, as he put it, 'Simply letting me down.'

*****

A beautiful life changer…

Kathy & Mark and their dog Bonzo

I wasn't all that fussed about getting a dog, but my husband Mark had grown up with dogs and was really keen to get another one after we got married. I had always had a bit of a fear of dogs, especially large ones, but I knew how much Mark wanted one so we made the decision to get one. Mark had always wanted a Labrador, and I had always had a fondness for Dachshunds, also known as 'sausage dogs', but we needed to find a dog that would suit our lifestyle as we both worked.

One day, Mark had heard about the plight of some retired racing Greyhounds that desperately needed homes as their apparent alternative was that their lives would be brought to an abrupt end. So many of them needed a home and people just simply did not realise what loving pets they make; they are real couch potatoes who can sleep for up to 18 hours a day and, contrary to popular belief, don't need much exercise. This sounded perfect for our working lifestyle so we looked into it further. We logged on to a Retired Greyhound Trust and had a look at some of the dogs up for adoption. They were all adorable and the more we read about what placid loving dogs they were, we made our mind up, we were going to get a Greyhound!

We chose three dogs that stood out for us and went over there to see if we could meet them and take them for a walk. We were told the first one on the list would be too young for us as we both work. We suggested Bonzo, a gorgeous black boy, who was second on our list and we thought looked really sweet and had been in a home previously. So out came Bonzo and we took him for a walk. That was it – he was adorable and that was it sewn up! We decided we would like him to be our dog. He had the height of a Labrador and the length of a sausage dog, so in actual fact we got the dog of our dreams – a cross between both our favourite breeds, and little did we know how quickly we would fall in love with him, and Greyhounds as a breed in general.

A couple of weeks later we went back to pick Bonzo up to take him home with us. I was initially still a bit nervous; because I was worried I might be scared when I was on my own with him. What a joke that was; Bonzo was the most gentle, placid dog you could ever meet. He completely cured my fear of dogs. Bonzo got under our skin so quickly that we were quite shocked how quickly we fell in love with him. We had already booked a holiday and a couple of weekends away before we got Bonzo so that first year he had a couple of visits to the kennels, but we missed him so much that we said, "That is it! He's had his time in the kennels now, no more!" And that was the last time he went back. He simply came away on all our holidays, weekends away; basically anywhere we could take him he would come with us. He had years of camping, cottages and finally caravanning with us throughout the UK. He became such a well-travelled dog and he loved it. He got so excited going on his holidays, doing his little twirls in the living room when Mark was loading up the car ready for us to go. It was adorable to see him grinning away. We were besotted with our beautiful boy!

It is probably a fitting scenario that we very sadly lost Bonzo whilst we were all away on holiday together in the North of England. We had been back and forth to the vets for a couple of weeks beforehand as he had started reverse sneezing and then later on, vomiting. The vets had given him antibiotics to treat him for bronchitis. They did an X-ray and blood tests to rule out a tumour in his chest as we told them he seemed to have also lost weight too, which we were worried about. The X-ray came back clear and we were told that the weight loss was down to age and muscle loss. Waiting for the results was terrifying and we were so relieved that there was nothing more seriously wrong with him than a severe case of bronchitis. We went off on our holiday armed with more antibiotics and Bonzo seemed to be improving, we started to relax and look forward to our holiday after a very scary couple of weeks.

A few days into our holiday, Bonzo started violently vomiting and it was heart-breaking to see. We had never seen Bonzo ill before these last couple of weeks, he had always been so healthy. We phoned the emergency vets and he said that this did not sound like bronchitis to him and for us to bring him in to him first thing the next morning. He had a blood test and an ultrasound and was very quickly diagnosed with a liver tumour. We were just numb with shock. They did not think that it had spread but would need to do a CT scan to be sure and felt that, as it was contained to one place, that if it could be removed he could go on for another couple of years as all his other organs were in fine working order. We had three choices – to put him to sleep, to give him tablets to ease the vomiting but we would lose him very soon anyway, or to give him the chance to have a CT scan and if it had not spread, then remove the tumour. We just had to give him the chance.

The next day Bonzo had the CT scan. It looked like it had not spread but they could not be completely sure until they opened him up. The surgeon said we were stuck between a rock and a hard place but he would advise surgery to be able to give him a chance. Our emotions were all over the place. We felt terrified but we just felt sure that our Bonzo was a tough cookie and would get through this.

We then received the phone call that quite simply broke our hearts. The operation had been going so well, they were only about ten minutes from the end of removing the tumour when Bonzo had a bleed. They tried to save him but he had lost too much blood to survive and passed away on 18th September 2014.

Words cannot describe how we felt. We just simply could not believe what had happened. Our beautiful boy had gone! How could this have happened? We were in total and utter shock. We had not even had chance to say goodbye to Bonzo. Our hearts were well and truly broken. We drove over to see him and to say goodbye. Seeing him lying on the operating table was just the most distressing thing. We kissed and cuddled him and just did not want to leave him. We literally sobbed our hearts out.

We had Bonzo cremated the next day and took him home with us where he belonged. Our home and our lives just felt so empty and so very sad without him. He was basically our life. Everything we did revolved around him and what he could do with us, and if he couldn't, then we wouldn't do it. It felt like a small part of us died with Bonzo that day.

I had recently become friendly with a lady at work who does spiritual readings, I had never had one of these done but was always fascinated by it all. I started to Google on the Internet to see if there was anything about if animals go to Heaven when they die and came across Jackie's website. It looked a brilliant website and had celebrities all singing Jackie's praises. To be honest, I was very sceptical and thought how can you actually speak to animals, especially ones that had passed away? Saying that, the reviews all seemed so real and when I mentioned it to my husband, we both said what have we got to lose? We can give it a try and hope. We knew that Jackie only needed a photo and Bonzo's name, age, how long we had him and when he had passed over.

We were still very emotional on the night of the reading, but straight away Jackie put us at ease with her lovely friendly manner and just started providing information to us from Bonzo as it came through to her.

Jackie first said that Bonzo told her he's very gentle but liked to have fun! This is so true. He was the gentlest of dogs. Our nieces, our friend's children and even myself all had a fear of dogs, but Bonzo was so gentle and sweet that he just made you fall in love with him instantly. But the best thing was his real cheeky side. He would have a really mad five minutes and start doing a 'loop the loop' and tearing around, with us holding our hands over our eyes thinking he would crash into something. Amazingly, he could stop on the spot and never bumped into anything.

Jackie then said he said he was lovely looking! Blimey Bonzo, bit bashful there eh boy? He once came third in the most handsome dog competition at a dog show one year on holiday, and everywhere we went people would often come up and say how beautiful he was. Jackie said to us that it seemed as if he looked at himself in a mirror. He did! We used to catch him checking himself out in the hall mirror! Now I know dogs aren't supposed to be able to see themselves in mirrors but they also aren't supposed to be able to talk, but Jackie's blown theories straight out of the window!

He then moved on to tell Jackie that he had an internal problem – something began to grow!! He knew how sad we were. He didn't think the onset was terribly long, just a matter of weeks. He knows we were so shocked and upset – we just didn't expect it! He said he was very brave but nothing could have been done. We couldn't have undone what was going wrong. He said he lost weight very quickly, and told Jackie that it had spread. Even if it had been removed, it wouldn't have worked. He told Jackie that he had also been treated for an infection! We sat there just saying "Oh my God! This is incredible!" This is really Bonzo!

He then went on to mention a small little dog, a very playful little dog! Fun! Fun! Straight away we realised this was my brother's dog. Bonzo and her have known each other since she was a pup and they loved each other. Bonzo again used to show his gentle side in that he would let her lie in his bed (and he would end up in her tiny bed with his long legs dangling out!), and drink from his bowl and eat his treats. They also used to have fun running on beaches together.

Bonzo then showed Jackie that he had a problem with his right hind leg and his foot at some point too. Also his kneecap had a trauma at some point too. His right hind leg was the leg that Bonzo went lame on from his racing days and the reason he retired at age four.

He then went on to tell Jackie that when we got him there were originally quite a few dogs up for rescue. He said there was a white dog there that was his buddy. We think this might have been a Greyhound called Caspar who we actually met when there was a meet up for all the rehomed retired Greyhounds. We were talking to a family there who had a pure white Greyhound called Caspar. Little did we know this had been Bonzo's buddy.

He then told Jackie that when he came to live with us he was like, "I died and went to Heaven!!" Jackie said she had never heard a dog in Heaven actually say those words before. We just went all gooey! How adorable of him to say such a thing. He loves us just as much as we love him!

Bonzo told Jackie that we still have his collar and that we had him cremated. This is true and we have Bonzo's urn with his collar around it. He said that we are looking for a nice picture of him to put beside it. He said that he thinks my picture is going to be beautiful and actually told Jackie that lying down like this with my legs crossed is a good look! Ha! There he goes again.

Bonzo then started laughing about his name "Bonzo". He said he liked it but that he thinks he should have had a name like "Prince" as he has a presence. This made us chuckle again!

He said he was not a harm to anyone and that Dad used to walk him more, but said that Dad's a bit lost now, and keeps thinking, "Come on, it's time to go walking!" This is true – Mark has continued to do his afternoon walk as he feels so lost without walking

Bonzo as part of his daily routine. Continuing to do his walk that they used to do together helps him feel close to Bonzo.

Bonzo then went on to say that he thinks we will get another Greyhound but this time it will be a girl – and pointed to the face as if she will have dots or spots on her face. This is really spooky as we had volunteered to walk retired Greyhounds the weekend before doing the reading. We aren't ready to get another dog yet, as for us it is too soon as we are still so raw after losing Bonzo and we had said we might possibly get another Greyhound around April. We asked if he would be upset if we got another dog eventually, as we would never want to try and replace him (that would be impossible!) to which he said to Jackie, "Do I look upset? Volunteering is wonderful because these dogs crave companionship."

Jackie then asked us if we took a rucksack out with us when we went out for the day – we surely did. We used to load Bonzo's water bottle, coat and picnic rug into it. Bonzo then told Jackie that he could not have asked for more. His racing days were part of his life and he enjoyed it, then it went wrong physically on his right hind leg. He said some of the dogs didn't enjoy the racing but Bonzo did and his racing track record proved this... he won 10 out of his 56 races. He told Jackie he was very loving to the other dogs and that he had quite a good social life. This made us giggle, we could just imagine him lapping it all up, bless him!

He said on the whole he was quite a healthy dog; he had some limps but had not really been ill. This is why it came as such a shock to us to see him being so sick, especially in those couple of weeks as we always thought he was indestructible. We told Jackie that we had been so worried that the flea treatment we had given him might have caused his tumour as he became very poorly a couple of days afterwards. He told Jackie that he had a tumour and anything toxic highlighted it. In a way it was a blessing because the flea stuff highlighted it like, "Oops something's going on!" He said that he had had flea treatment in the past and that tumours don't just grow like that anyway. He said, "Please, no guilt! No guilt!" He then said, "If Mark had head lice and I shampooed his head with shampoo, would I think I'd given him a liver tumour? Er No!" We all started laughing, and then he asked, "Did you like my head lice story?" which really made us giggle! What a funny fella Bonzo actually was! If only we had been able to talk to him when he was still alive, it would have been hilarious!

Bonzo then showed Jackie a bus. He used to see buses passing along the main road before crossing into the park. He told Jackie that from the main road pavement to cross into the park is 25 strides, but we said we actually thought it was not as many as that. We just had to check this out and we have since counted this and it is exactly 25 strides!

He then said "You did me proud!! You did everything right for me!! I taught you true dog love! Those words choked us up a bit I can tell you. Bonzo then made reference to the small dog again. He said to say "Hello" to her from him and explain to her what has happened when we next see her as she might be worried. What a thoughtful dog he still is.

We did not want the session to end and asked if he would mind if we did this again. He said we can come and talk to him anytime. He can hear what we say. He knows he is on our mind as we go to sleep and as we wake up.

Jackie says he then really smiles and says "I was the lucky one!" We said, " No, we were!" and then he says it again. Jackie says it's like we are competing with each other. We thought how lovely of him to say this to us. A few days later, I suddenly remembered a conversation we had previously had with Mark's mum when she had said that Bonzo was a lucky boy with the life he had with us, and we had corrected her and said "No we were the lucky ones!" And this was what he had been repeating back to us in reverse. Unbelievable!

Bonzo then mentioned the white dog again which Jackie thinks has also passed away. We believe this is Caspar. He said they are running around together again. I later checked the Retired Greyhound website memorial page, Caspar had died about three years earlier and he had been about a year younger than Bonzo and had definitely been in the kennels the same time as him. Wow!

He then asked, "Is somebody writing a poem?" We were a bit puzzled as we are definitely no poets and the only thing we could think he was referring to was that we were trying to find the right words for our memorial message for him for the retired Greyhound website. So I said, "Does he want us to?" To which he replied, "She's asking me?" "Okay, I think it should be called, " Bonzo the Black Prince!" Guess who has since gone on to write a poem for Bonzo's memorial message? Yes, me (Kathy) and it has the title "Bonzo Our Beautiful Black Prince!"

We asked him if he thought we will meet up again one day with him. He said "Yes, and then you can kiss my head! I'm safe, I'm in doggy land!"

Well, we have to say this just has to be the most amazing surreal experience ever. We just simply did not want the session to end and cannot thank Jackie enough. To hear that our wonderful boy loves us as much as we love him was incredible, and to hear his sense of humour, well that was simply something else. To think of all the qualities we love about him, who would have known that we also had such a comedian on our hands? We always knew Bonzo was special, but he now seems even more special, if that were ever possible?

We will love and miss Bonzo forever, but we now know, thanks to Jackie, that we will see him again one day, and we can kiss him on the head! Until then, sweet boy, have lots of fun running around with Caspar and we will see you again one day!

(An update... They did get their new Greyhound: A white girl, complete with those spots, named Angel – definitely Heaven sent. Well done Bonzo.)

*****

Such a loving and special girl...

Clwyd and his cat Topsi

We had lost my mother to cancer in March 1994 and of course the family was devastated, I was 19 at the time. But in September of that year, a cat suddenly appeared in our lives having been given to my sister by her work colleague. She was a tortoiseshell colour with a white face and belly, a truly beautiful looking cat. She was thought to be about a year old and came in to our house without a shred of fear. She walked with her tail and head held high, so lightly on her feet, inquisitively and confidently taking everything in her stride, and looked at us with those big yellow eyes. If, as the old adage goes, the eyes are the windows to the soul, then hers were a huge picture window. Her eyes reflected wisdom as well as humour. My father took to her immediately as we all did. She doted on us and we doted on her. We named her Topsi and soon Topsi and I became inseparable.

On her first night we put her in the cellar with a box, blanket and a toy, but she was straight up the stairs after us, meowing away at the door. We carried her down again, this time leaving the light on, but up she came again meowing away. In the end we let her sleep on my father's large bed, hoping this would calm her down. It worked! Topsi relaxed and lay down near my dad's feet. Soon the little one slept, snuggled safely in the folds of the duvet.

A little later we took her to the vets (a trip all animals I believe are not that keen on) to get her jabs, and neutered. We were worried how she would react but, bless her; she was as good as gold, again taking everything in her stride. She came home feeling very groggy after the anaesthesia and she slept for hours. She was unsteady on her feet for a while and, understandably a tad upset after her 'ordeal', she would go into hiding for hours. Eventually, all was forgiven.

Sometimes she would come running at full speed up to my feet and stop suddenly. She'd stare right into my eyes, as if she wanted me to chase her, then doing a 180 degree turn off she went to hide. This was her favourite game in her younger days. As the years grew, our bond grew stronger and she had a close loving relationship with everyone. She would love strangers coming to the house, and would trot to the door whenever the doorbell rang. She loved her food and twice a week I would give her a treat she loved: either chicken or tuna with broccoli and a drop of olive oil.

In wintertime her favourite spot was always in front of our gas fire, either in the living room or the back room; but her best time of the year was the summer. She loved lazing in the sun or in the greenhouse, lying on her side in the garden with her legs splayed out in front of her; I called it the 'Jabba the Hut' pose. She was never really was interested in hunting birds, although loved to look at the them in the trees with her little mouth going, making that funny noise cats do, and even the neighbour's dog didn't scare her at all.

When Topsi was about five we adopted a kitten from a farmer friend of mine. After the initial nervousness they both got on well, although the new cat was like a small ball of madness, climbing up curtains, jumping about, even knocking over the Christmas tree, so we called her Crazy. Years ticked gloriously by and both cats drifted into their senior years.

Last November, on a freezing cold night, a tiny kitten appeared on our doorstep, obviously abandoned. We took her in, and she took to Topsi immediately. As Topsi lay in her bed in front of the fire, the little one, Eli, pushed in and shared the basket; again Topsi adopted the little cat under her wing. Did Eli think of Topsi as a mother figure, who knows?

A few months later, Topsi had an eye ulcer and despite extensive treatment the vet had no choice but to take out the eye. It was heart-breaking to see dear

Topsi with a bandage across her face, but after a while she became used to her disability and was getting on fine until we started to notice she had trouble standing on her own. She was still drinking, eating and using the cat litter, but she became very weak quite quickly, so we rang the vet and they came to our house, as we were very worried about this. The vet decided she would need a blood test, but warned us that at 21 years of age she might be coming to the end of her life. The vet took her away to his surgery and would phone us the next morning after the result. When the phone rang, my heart was beating hoping for the best, but fearing the worst. The diagnosis was very bad, her kidneys weren't working, her red blood cell count was very low, and he said it would be kinder to put Topsi to sleep. I won't go into details, but saying goodbye to her, stroking her head she looked at me with those big soulful eyes as the vet euthanized her, was one of the most traumatic days of my life. But she went very quickly, released from her elderly and ailing body.

The loss hit me hard, both emotionally and physically. I was devastated, felt nauseous for days and was an emotional wreck. I felt like a zombie. She may have been a cat but I tell you now, the loss hits you like a ton of bricks. They say grief is the price of loving, very true. She had become a part of the family, my family. Everyone who cares deeply about an animal must eventually endure the death of their special friend. It is one of the most painful experiences we endure.

A short time later, I was browsing the web one night about spiritualism, and Googled what happens when we die? Do we have souls? And do animals have souls too? I came across animal communication for the first time and initially was sceptical about it; it seemed too fantastic to be true. I did some research and Jackie Weaver's name popped up and had glowing references so I bought a few of her books on the subject. After reading them, I had grown a bit more convinced there was something to it. After emailing Jackie and paying the fee, I sent her two pictures of Topsi sitting alone, and week later she called me.

Jackie was very friendly and spoke about Topsi's life with us and said many things that were true. Examples being about how Topsi suddenly appeared in our lives and she didn't feel nervous at all, which was true, and that she loved the garden and would lie on her side sunbathing. Also that she was friendly and not scared of strangers, true again. She said Topsi felt very loved by us and she had a good life, yes. She said she felt Topsi was very healthy all her life until the last week, which was exactly right. She said Topsi liked to watch birds and make a little noise when she did, again true. To my surprise, Jackie asked me if I have two other cats, indeed I have. How could Jackie have known that? She said the young one is wild, and the older cat was wild too, to begin with, but settled down and has started to drink a lot of water recently. Again, this is all correct. Jackie then said Topsi loved it when the coal was being put on. For a second I couldn't understand what this meant and told her we don't have a coal fire we have two gas fires. A few seconds later it dawned on me what she meant... we do have artificial coal on both our gas fires that we have in the living room and back room. Topsi loved to lie in front of them and gaze at the glowing 'coal'.

Jackie said Topsi is happy where she is and that occasionally a dog would come to her spot, but would then go away when Topsi would raise her back to mark her patch! That made me laugh. Then Jackie told me something that made me kind of flinch, Topsi was showing her an image of a cemetery. I didn't know what this meant, Jackie suggested this could mean I am comfortable with spiritualism and accept death as part of nature. This is very true, as a Christian I do believe in the afterlife, which is the corner stone of faith. I once heard in a sermon that Christianity is not about the cross but is about the empty tomb, the resurrection. And if humans have a soul why can't animals that we share our lives with have one too? As Pope John II said, "Animals possess a soul and men must love and feel solidarity with our smaller brethren. Animals are as near to God as men are." And the word 'animal' comes from the Latin word meaning 'soul'.

Yes it was a strange, but wonderful and rewarding experience. Whatever your beliefs, or if you have none at all is up to you, but I believe that death isn't the end, our bodies are simply shells that contain our souls. We are born, we live our life, and we pass on to the after life or are re-born. Jackie has a God given gift. I cherish the time I had with Topsi and thank Jackie for giving me an insight into her life, and her life in spirit too.

*****

A bit of a shock for such a gentle girl...

Ian and his dog Jess

I have known Jackie personally for many years. I was, in fact, witness to her courageous battle with cancer as I lived close by. I have to say, to see someone at 'death's door' to survive and then her wonderful gift become apparent has been inspiring to say the least. Jackie used her animal communication skills to help me with my dog, Henry, who was featured in her *Animal Talking Tales* book, so when my lovely yellow Labrador, Jess, had a sudden behavioural problem, I knew exactly who to call.

Jess is eight-years-old and, as Jackie relayed, is the most adorable girl and a wonderful family pet. She has a good head on her shoulders and is no trouble at all. This is why I was so perplexed as to why she had been going out in the enclosed back yard for years, but now she point blankly was refusing to do so. None of the family could persuade her to go out there, not even for food! So we were at a loss, so over to Jackie to ask her 'personally'.

Jackie immediately mentioned a night that was raining very heavily. This is the UK so we laughed as this is the 'norm', but Jackie said Jess was insisting on showing this horrendous pouring rain as if this was relevant. Although Jackie had been to my house she went on to ask me to clarify various images that Jess was passing her. Jackie asked if we had a washing line that was attached to what seemed to be a very ornate, Victorian-style iron drainpipe. I confirmed there was a drainpipe exactly like that, and a washing line. Jackie then said that she was given the sound, as if maybe an end was touching it off and on and creating a sort of 'tick tick' 'ping ping' sound, and then a golden spray of fizzing sparks, like fireworks. Jackie said that she has no idea why that would worry such a sensible dog but, like a jigsaw puzzle, she would keep going and see if we could put the bits together.

Jackie then asked Jess to show her how she felt about going out into the yard, and even though the other dogs went out without an issue, she seemed terrified. She was! We even tried to carry her out, but she resisted and struggled so much that we had to give up as she was so stressed. Jess then volunteered, "There are a lot of electrical units on the other side of the wall." This was correct, as it is a large utility room complete with many devices including a large central heating unit. Jackie then asked if it was possible that the 'line' she had seen could be an electrical source coming in from the outside into the utility room by the metal down pipe? I had to admit, I did not know but would get my handyman to go and have a look and would phone her back in a few minutes. Oh my goodness! The handyman came back and said that the wiring did indeed come through the wall at the metal drainpipe, but, to our horror, someone had done a 'botch' job... There was another wire, now 'disconnected' by simply being folded over and covered in insulating tape. The rain had eventually washed this tape down and exposed a live wire! Now all became clear: when it was pouring with heavy rain this was enough for a live supply for the sparks to fly out of the pipe with a lot of fizzing and crackling as well. Certainly it would have been enough to a give poor Jess a terrible fright. No wonder she would not step out there whatever we tried.

Jackie, as usual, said that she could not promise to change Jess's mind but would one: thank her for letting us know of the danger, and two: let her know that it is perfectly safe now.

I thanked Jackie for her help and amazing insight. To quote the handyman, who is not really *au fait* with psychic matters, 'To be fair, how she got that I have no idea but she was right!' I said I would let her know how we got on persuading Jess that all was safe. We did in the end but it did take a while. Fortunately there was another way to get into the yard so we brought her back into the house that way. Eventually the yard became the usual safe place it was.

Thank you Jackie and, although it was so desperate to see a young person so ill, it shows it was really not your time and I can see why you were saved.

*****

The bravest girl ever...

Susan and her dog Coco

Coco found me on March 19th 2006, the day after my birthday. Myself, and my husband Ian, went to look at a litter of Chocolate Labrador puppies; they were beautiful, full of life, with more bounces than a tennis ball. They were full of excitement and wonder and I had to make a really hard decision, which baby do I choose? My heart said, "Take all of them", but my inner self smiled and said, "be sensible; you came for one puppy and so choose one." There I was with six pairs of beautiful eyes looking at me with tails and bottoms wagging all over the place and then, another caught my eye. Sat in the corner at the back, head slightly down, but looking directly at me... The hairs on the back of my neck stood up and I fell in love, I knew it had to be this one. She wasn't the liveliest puppy, she was definitely the smallest of the litter, tiny in comparison, but there was an instant connection and in that moment Coco had found me.

I didn't know at the time, she would change my life forever. She was simply amazing, full of love for everything and everybody. Whoever came to visit would be greeted with her favourite 'baby' (a soft toy), complete with wagging bottom and tail that were never still. She didn't care much for balls or chewy bones; she liked soft toys, her beanies and babies were cared for and treasured.

Coco underwent many surgeries in her life, with the first before the age of one! Little did I know, she had found a pencil, chewed, and then ate it. She was at puppy class the same afternoon, one moment she was playing and the next she had collapsed. It was the scariest moment of my life to date, we rushed her to our vets and she was taken straight into surgery. How a pencil could cause such a problem, but it did certainly did! We decided at this point that she would be with us wherever we went, and I would watch her like a hawk.

The holidays abroad stopped and we purchased a caravan. She loved it and was the perfect traveller. She would lay on her caravan blanket with her head looking out the door surveying her surroundings. When we went to the beach she would rush in to the sea, dip her head below the water, and stop suddenly as soon as the water reached her chest. Then she would bounce out of the sea, roll in the sand and the process would start again. We were so close it was incredible – wherever I was, Coco was. I finished at 8 o'clock when I was on a late shift at work and she would be waiting at the gate for me; she never missed, rain or snow she was always waiting. Ian said she knew it was time; she would get up and go to the door, and look at the handle until he opened the door – she just knew Mummy was coming home!

We were on holiday for her second birthday, so we wore party hats; yes even Coco! We had sandwiches and birthday cakes and then it was time to open her presents. She did this ever so gently and guess what? Yes, another baby to add to the ever-growing collection. Every time I think of these times I laugh to myself and smile so broadly; she was my baby and I loved her so much. Coco was a gentle girl, carefree with a love of life, but at the age of three her life changed.

She started limping, and after many visits to the vets and X-rays she began the wave of six operations on her back legs that would span the next three years. She never stopped wagging her tail and never stopped loving us, she just soldiered on and got on with it – she was incredible and oozed happiness in spite of everything. I had almost ten wonderful, amazing years with her. We would sit on the floor at night together, read books together; she was my best friend and we knew each other inside out.

As she got older, the past problems started catching up with her. She slowed down and I started to worry. Only when she had previously undergone surgery had I thought about the end. How would I cope without her? I sat and had a conversation with her, and asked her to let me know when it was time. I cried like a baby throughout. Sunday 27th December, I came downstairs in the morning and instantly knew something was wrong... she was lain on her bed and would not move her head, and if she tried she cried out. We took her to the vets and she was given injections to ease the pain. To our immense relief she seemed to bounce back a few hours later, but the following day she was the same. She was shaking from head to tail, so again we went back to the vets for more injections, anti-inflammatories. I came home from work on Sunday 31st December and Coco was on her bed again, head down and trembling. I got on the floor to her level and looked into her eyes, it was then that I knew; we had reached the end of our adventure. The light had gone and as she looked at me, I instantly knew what I had to do. Bravely I called the out of hours vets, explained the situation and agreed to take her straight down. I looked at Coco and said, "It is time baby girl" and she got off her bed walked out the back door and stood at the car – she had answered my question. The vet looked at Coco and agreed that I had made the right decision. I lay on the floor with her, put my arms around her and said, "It's night-night time baby girl, I love you, close your eyes, it's okay." I felt her take one last breath and she was gone. No more pain, and it was a beautiful end for her. I hugged her for a while, and told her that I loved her.

I had never felt so alone in my entire life. What do I do without her? Have I made the right decision? How will I ever know? It was then that I searched the Internet and found Jackie. I sent her an email and explained I had just lost my baby. I needed to know that Coco was okay and that I had made the right decision for her. I had the reading with Jackie, I was so nervous about what Coco would have to say, but Jackie literally blew me away in the time that followed.

Coco had said she was slightly off colour and she had been panting a lot, but she was not paralysed. Something had moved and she was in severe discomfort. Coco said she didn't even need a lead, and this was so true in the last year we walked together. She enjoyed our chill out time, and I always knew when it was 'wee wee' time for her. This made me chuckle as I would always say to her, "Come on baby girl, it's wee wee time." She said she had the 'bestest' life, and she was a 'brave soldier'. That final week she had given up, I know because she could not be carried in and out. I asked Coco if I had made the right decision and she replied with, "YOU KNEW ME and I didn't want to hurt anymore. It was a blessed goodbye. Your pain will ease, so stop feeling guilty and stop crying. I Love you." She also added at this point that she wanted the biggest picture on the wall. I smiled as I explained to Jackie, that it was already in place. A wave of calm washed over me at this moment and I knew she would be with me forever. I had one more question to ask and I was really worried about the answer I would receive, but it doesn't end here...

Three days before my reading, an advert for Chocolate Labrador puppies caught my eye. Although I know that there is not a living creature on this earth that can ever replace Coco, she had given me so much love I felt the need to pass this on. I searched the Internet and found a puppy, who was actually a Golden Labrador Retriever. In the photograph she was looking straight at the camera; I felt like she was looking at me just like Coco on our first meeting. I knew it was the right decision so I contacted the breeder. When she replied the following morning, she informed me that that little girl was actually reserved and all the puppies had gone with the exception of two chocolate ones. I said I didn't want another chocolate and thanked her.

I couldn't stop thinking about it and Ian finally said, we should go and look, if it's not right you will know. I called her back and said we would be with her in two hours. When we arrived, there they were: two beautiful chocolate Labrador puppies. I picked one up, she was adorable, but I looked at the Breeder and said, "I'm sorry I can't." She asked why and I explained about Coco. She understood straight away due to losing her own dog a few months previous. She asked me to wait a minute while she had a quick word with her husband. He then disappeared but walked back in with the puppy from the photograph! The breeder explained that although this puppy had been reserved they wanted to offer me the choice of having her instead. It was easy... I had no qualms about it and we left with this gorgeous puppy who we called Elsa! On the way home we could not get over the fact that we had gone to look at two chocolate Labradors, but had come away with the puppy I had wanted in the first place, and we would have missed her if we had not taken the chance – fate must surely have lent a hand here.

So, back to Coco and Jackie... Coming up to the end of my reading, as I was just about to ask a question, when Jackie said to me, that she had a really bold statement from Coco which was, 'A retriever needs rescuing; she is Heaven sent.' The exact question for Coco was about the fact that I had found another puppy so soon after saying goodbye to her and hoped she was not cross. My question had been answered, before I had even asked her! Coco knew, and she had sent her to me. (Regarding her needing to be 'rescued', I am sure it would have been a lovely home, but maybe another animal may not have accepted her or some other problem. We will never know but Elsa is so special and she was most definitely Heaven sent.) Coco said she is going to be a wonderful girl, and I needed a break with a healthy dog. I asked if I would ever physically see or feel Coco, and she answered that when it's right, I will feel her paw on my left shoulder and that you will see 'me' in Elsa.

I will never be able to thank Jackie enough for giving me the chance to speak with Coco, or for the overwhelming love and joy I now feel and I have emailed Jackie to say exactly that. She replied very quickly to point out another amazing coincidence, although Jackie says there is no such thing! On the morning of our reading she had put a post on her Facebook page about her next book (this one) coming out. She had quickly searched the Internet to find a cute dog picture, and guess what it was? A Golden Retriever puppy! You just could not make it up!

Jackie communicated many things to me that no other person apart from me could ever know. Coco will be in my thoughts daily and my heart forever. Thank you with all my heart.

*****

A little boy who brought so much love and joy...

Michael & Pearl and their cat Oliver

Oliver came to us as a kitten at five months old. He was a sweet looking little tabby and white, but unwanted by his previous owner. We had just lost

Mollie, our elderly and very sick cat, so it took me a few days to be drawn to Oliver.

My wife Pearl had no such reservations – it was love at first sight, and Oliver was about to drown in a sea of love and affection. Pearl was so worried that Oliver could get lost when first allowed out on his own, that she bought a very small harness that fitted Oliver securely. The village dog walkers must have been surprised when joined by a lady walking her cat at the end of a lead! Oliver was happy to go out like that and in later years, he would sit on the drive and wait for Pearl to put on her jacket and shoes, then the pair of them would go off for walks together, no longer needing a harness I might add.

On one annual visit to the vets, they revealed that Oliver had a slight heart murmur, but it did not seem to be a problem and slipped to the back of our minds.

Oliver loved to be outdoors and could frequently be seen high in the trees around our property watching all that was going on below. Even if it poured with rain Oliver would find a dry spot under the hedge rather than come indoors. Oliver was always a very quiet and undemanding cat, so quiet that we thought he was perhaps nervous.

When Oliver was about four years old we came across a magazine article that gave details of Jackie Weaver and her work. Curiosity aroused we contacted Jackie to see if we could learn anything about our Oliver. It was a really surprising experience.

One of the many things we learnt from Oliver via Jackie was that he considered himself a passive cat and certainly *not* a nervous one. This was borne out by his love of fireworks! If a neighbour had a firework party in his garden, Oliver would invite himself, climbing a nearby tree, he would be totally unperturbed by the explosions and was fascinated by the bright lights.

With Oliver we had a life of love and bliss – he was a joy to both of us. Oliver was eleven when we noticed he was having trouble with his breathing. We made an appointment with our vet and how fortunate it turned out that he specialised in cardiology. The vet gently lifted Oliver from his carrier placed him on the table and listened to his heart. Suddenly, he scooped Oliver up and rushed from the room, calling over his shoulder, "Let's hope I can save him." We were left in complete shock - we had no idea that Oliver was so unwell.

When the vet returned he said that Oliver was in an oxygen chamber as his lungs were full of fluid and it was touch and go. We were advised that to save Oliver he would need to be sedated and his lungs drained. It was worrying, for in his weakened state, Oliver might not survive. Four hours later we received a phone call telling us that although they had almost lost him twice, Oliver had survived and we could take him home. Words could not describe our relief.

Over the next four months Oliver's breathing fluctuated enormously and at some points he was being rushed to the oxygen chamber on an almost daily basis. I have to say; he was amazing throughout and would bounce back to his happy self and the care, kindness and attention Oliver received from the vet and his team was wonderful.

Sadly came the day when one of the vets said he needed a 'little chat'. Such a simple phrase but with such awful consequences. How do you describe the sadness and despair of letting an adored pet go? We had no choice and we left the vets overwhelmed with grief. It was so final; our beautiful boy was gone.

I know a card of condolence from the vet is standard practice, but the vet and his team must have taken Oliver to their hearts, for his card of condolence arrived with a beautiful bouquet of flowers as well. We were so very touched.

We were so fortunate to be aware of Jackie from our previous communication so the day after Oliver passed we booked an appointment and waited as patiently as possible. Our concern was to know that Oliver was well and that he understood why, and with many tears, we let him go.

Jackie rang very promptly, Pearl answered the phone and after a polite greeting I was really surprised to hear Pearl laugh and see her smile. She settled quickly in to what was obviously a very happy and extremely long telephone call.

With Jackie's help we learnt that Oliver was now well and happy and he knew it was right. He said he was ready to go as he was becoming weaker, which in his words was, 'just body failure'. He sweetly told us that although it was a sad demise it was not a painful one.

So many things Jackie could not possibly have known left Pearl in no doubt she was talking to Oliver. We had started a memory box for Oliver and he was aware of this. He was well known to our neighbours and he said he was aware people were asking after him and stressed that he had truly loved his dad.

Oliver told us he was aware of how much he had been loved and that his life with us had been very happy. He assured Pearl he would be waiting for us when our turn came, but for now he would look after us from spirit. He said we would feel him jump on the bed at night (this has happened and several times too.)

He also mentioned a black cat, this cat we call Squeaky who had run away from his home and was living in our hedge. Much to Oliver's disgust, Squeaky made a very determined and successful effort to move in with us. Oliver's comment from spirit that Squeaky would eat us out of house and home made us laugh as so true, this cat never stops eating!

Oliver mentioned the name Jessie, and Jackie said she felt maybe it was an animal spirit Oliver had met up with. We confirmed it was a cat who was his friend who passed the year before from cancer. The pair of them were very close and neighbours often told us what pleasure they got from watching them play together in the fields and gardens around our home. This knowledge gave us great pleasure.

Oliver requested that we light a candle for him and Spirit for all they had done for us. He closed the call by telling Pearl he was off to play now and that he could see the stars and they were very close!

The next day we went to a beautiful church in Ottery-St-Mary. The church was full of activity with cleaning and decorating readying it for Christmas. Being so inquisitive Oliver would have loved the atmosphere. We lit a candle, for Oliver and Spirit, said a brief prayer, and left the church smiling.

Oliver, through Jackie, had helped us enormously to cope with his loss.

*****

This is a poem I include in every book. It was given to me straight from spirit to try and help people who have to make the heart-wrenching decision. I hope it helps you, like it has so many others.

Letting Go

Your heart is bursting, searing with pain
That physical touch never to be had again
You only let them go because you so clearly care
They might not be here but they are surely up there.

You feel the pull and the tear of your heart
You feel torn inside and ripped apart
The enormity of choosing what best to do
It was done with your love, as they looked to you.

We don't enter into this without thought or care
We do it because the compassion is there
The choice to stop pain and distress of the one we love
Can only be guided by you and the Angels above.

Many spirits have come through and given me their word
Your tears of sorrow and distress they heard
But they are free and happy and hold no ill will
Whatever was wrong could not have been cured with a pill.

For the Love of Pets

The height of pain is a measuring device
It shows how deeply you felt throughout their life
With your love given for this most selfless act
They at least left this earth with their heart intact.

Now up yonder and free to roam
This is another level, like a new home
The day will come when you go up there too
They're ready and waiting to meet and embrace you.

If you truly did this from your genuine heart
You were so brave and helped them depart
Your love and courage was seen from above
This really was your strongest act of love.

If you could ask them now, what might they say?
"In my life, that was actually only one single day,
Please remember the rest, the joy, love and play,
For I look down from above and remember it that way."

As time has passed you may at last feel some ease
Maybe a pet has come for you to please
Animals are not selfish and want you to share
They left that space for another needing your love and care.

We are truly honoured to share in their space
Think back and let that smile adorn your face
The precious time you had could never be measured
Your lasting memories are of those you truly treasured.

Jackie Weaver 2009

*****

As mentioned in my foreword, I still have some stories written by me of cases that I have done. (The majority seem to be horse related but horses are amazing and can teach us so much.) Here are a few for you...

A Cruel Departure

I had spent a lovely few hours at one yard chatting to three horses, well, one pony and two horses to be precise. They were all so different; the pony was the family pet and a cheeky but honourable little chap. One horse had an, 'I'd rather do it my way or not at all' attitude, but the other was the crème de la crème of horses, he had been there, done it and got the tee-shirt! He chatted about his previous home where he had competed at top level. It is not often that horses show me bottles of champagne, but he did, coupled with rows and rows of red rosettes. He also showed me a picture of the biggest and poshest of horseboxes you would ever see! But, saying all that, he was having a more sedate life now, and was totally adored by his present owner. He told us that he really loved this personal home which was far more endearing to him than a professional yard.

I was now at the next call and standing in front of a young mare called Cinnamon, aptly named after her roan colour. I was quite surprised as it seemed I was going to be doing the communication with her husband rather than the lady who had booked it. I don't mean to sound sexist, but men normally tend to be very sceptical unless they have experienced it personally. My luck was in, her owners had done communication before with someone else so they knew how it worked and what to expect. I tuned in with this youngster who was rising five, and immediately was bombarded with this angst. She made me feel like I wanted to stamp my feet, and shout and cry like a child, 'Why me, why me, it is all so unfair!' I passed this over, and the owner nodded, saying that was her to a tee. Just at that point his wife appeared, introduced herself and I said I would just let Cinnamon rant and see why she felt like this.

The mare went on and on, and said she was not awkward, although people thought it of her, and this turned out to be mainly about her breaking process. The problem was, yes she was tricky, yes she was rather awkward but, unfortunately, an old joint injury was starting to hurt again. So this unwillingness to work was because of discomfort, but unfortunately looked like more behavioural problems. She was talking at speed, saying things to me as fast as I could repeat them, but we established that there was a problem breaking and, in the end, she had come home.

The next picture was of her hurtling round and round a stable but she looked like a foal. She then said, "Oh, I miss my mum, where is my mum?"

His wife looked so crestfallen, and she uttered, "I knew it was about this; my sister has always said the same." I got the background and, sadly, someone had recommended their method of weaning, which was to take mother out of the stable, hold the foal back, and shut all doors! Well, the obvious happened, this poor foal just screamed and cried for days. This set up terrible anxieties and a lack of trust in people, because if they can take away the most precious thing, her mum, then what else were they capable of? The owner felt dreadful and had realised that this was a big mistake and has never done it like that since. I hear a lot of similar stories and try to tell people, think of it like you yourself. Say, for example; the one you love has to leave you to go and live abroad – you would not like it, but if you had been told and had the time, then you could get used to it. You would also take that opportunity to say all you wanted to and, in the end, learn to accept it. Or, on the other hand, would you like to have it this way? You go into the house you have shared for months and whilst you are upstairs, someone drags her off. You come downstairs and you find there is... nothing! What's happened?! You cry, 'Is she okay, did she run away, does she not want me anymore? Please someone, tell me when I will see her again?' Done like that, do you think you would hear any answers? No, and the sad thing is people can't hear these innocents that are shouting the questions.

By now we had told Cinnamon her mother was well and this had been a mistake. She understood but said that she didn't think she would be able to work because of her leg problem. She showed me what looked like a curve in a bone, and this turned out to be where she had been operated on her hock, but, sadly, riding had actually caused inflammation in this damaged joint.

Her owners asked me to ask her what she wanted in life. Her answer – not to be ridden, but as she was very good looking and was well bred, she would love to have babies for them. It was promised there and then that next year she would visit the stallion and try for a foal and of course, thanks to this sad learning curve, the weaning would be done in the most thoughtful and least stressful way possible.

*****

Finding the Key

One Saturday in September 2009, I was sitting facing the entrance door at a holistic fair in North Wales, which I had worked at previously in March. I really do very few of the 'mind, body, spirit' type fairs, but going there is more like a friends reunion and full of good atmosphere. It also is a great excuse to get the caravan out, and walk our dog Sally over the many beautiful hills around there.

Many people think that these sorts of fairs are full of 'strange' people reading cards and fortune-telling. Yes, of course there are people that do clairvoyant and psychic work (it is certainly not 'strange' to me, after all, I am clairvoyant too and most people are embracing what I do!), but also there are many healing and alternative types of treatments and much more to experience there.

The great thing about these types of venues is that therapists tend to do taster sessions of what service they provide. So, for a small price you can decide for yourself what you think is beneficial or not. I was now surrounded by many interesting people and was organised with my table all set up ready so that people could sit down and have an animal reading.

It was about ten o'clock when a girl walked through the doorway and her face did one of those double take impressions then blurted out, "I saw you on TV yesterday!" which made me laugh out loud as it was such a surreal moment. I am just an everyday ordinary person who just happens to have been extremely lucky how my life has transformed. I laughed and said, "Please take a seat." She carried on oblivious to my suggestion, saying, "I just knew I had to come today, I just knew it, and when I saw you on TV I just knew you were the lady to help Ruby!"

She burbled away at about a hundred miles an hour telling me, "I am not from around here; I am from Yorkshire and I'm just here to visit some friends. Wow, how amazing is this?!" I smiled and asked her and her friend, Lindsay, to sit down so we could chat some more.

At these types of venues the last thing people expect is to find someone that can talk to their animals, but thanks to Kirsty and her enthusiastic comments, people were already filling their names and details in on my booking sheet.

Once Kirsty had got her breath back, and the look of shock had gone from her face, she sat down and introduced herself properly. She was only young (well comparative to me); I would hazard a guess at about twenty-five. She had travelled down with Lindsay from 'up North' where they share a flat and the dog in question, Ruby.

Ruby was a large female Doberman they had got from an animal rescue shelter about a year ago. I looked at a picture of her, which Kirsty had on her mobile phone. I tuned in with Ruby and she immediately told me how loving she was, but was very, very wary of strangers and men in particular.

She started 'throwing' me pictures of what looked like some horrible, domineering person bawling and aggressively pushing her about, and then gave me a picture of what looked like her following the walls inside a house. I asked the girls if she maybe did that inside the flat, like she was trying to look invisible, like blending into the walls? They recognised this instantly, but said that was when they first got her and that she rarely does it now.

Ruby then gave a completely opposite style of picture and this was of her lying fully stretched out over someone on a settee! They laughed as this was so right, but being a big dog they couldn't let her do it for long as she just totally squashed them, but it was such fun! Doberman dogs are big and strong and often weigh the same as a small person, so I totally understood why this affection-seeking mode had its limitations!

We covered various problems but the main one was beating their logical brains. They posed the question to me, 'Why, when Lindsay went out, did Ruby not bark or get upset, yet when Kirsty went out she would not settle and would bark and whine until Kirsty returned?' "Mmm," I thought, "This will be interesting," so I simply asked Ruby what was the difference between Lindsay going out and Kirsty doing the same?

"But she might not come back," was the worrying cry and I asked her to try and be clearer. Then she showed me a key and tried to get over to me that when the door wasn't locked that was the difference! I was not really sure I was picking this up correctly but passed it over anyway.

Kirsty and Lindsay discussed the locking process to see if we could make sense of what she was saying. They established that Lindsay went out to work early in the mornings for her day job and would simply lock the door and go. Also, during the day if Kirsty went out she would lock up behind her too. On the other hand, when Kirsty went to her part-time job in the evening, Kirsty would seldom have to lock the door as Lindsay was at home.

With that, Kirsty's eyes widened, and she exclaimed, "Oh no, I hardly ever take my keys, because I don't need to unlock the door to come back in!" Now this was starting to make sense. Logically, if you were not coming back to a house, why would you take your keys with you? Bingo! We had got it, and now I had to explain this to Ruby and ask what Kirsty could do to help re-assure her. Very simply she asked that every time Kirsty went out to show Ruby her key-ring, complete with the small stuffed toy that she visualised for me, and say, "Look, I have my keys, so I will be coming back."

We finished the chat and I said it was lovely to meet them and I hoped that Ruby would settle down. I got an update a few months later letting me know that although she was still barking, it was so much less and they could cope with it and hoped eventually it would peter out. Kirsty also said that it had made a huge difference to her and Lindsay just to hear what Ruby had to say and was so glad to have been guided in my direction. It had been such a special day for them, and I laughed about the 'TV recognition' which although was still surreal, made it an extra special one for me too.

*****

Coming and Going

It was the middle of the day and I got an email through from an owner saying that a chiropractor had been on the yard and had suggested that she try me, and it was very, very urgent. I emailed straight back, and we got everything organised within the hour, and then I called her.

She was in tears and, to be honest, it was quite a difficult conversation to hold as I didn't know what she was expecting but, between the tears, she sounded rather annoyed! I explained that her horse, Hugo, could also hear what we were saying, which caused a bit of confusion as she was worried because she was not at the yard. I explained that it was immaterial as I work to the subconscious so you do not need to be near them, and also they can be doing as they please at the same time too.

Hugo was a beautiful grey horse and was about twelve years old. He was happy to chat and said that he was genuine and, with that, his owner interrupted with, "Well, that might be his opinion!" I quickly reminded her we were in a three-way conversation and shall I just see what he says? She reluctantly agreed, so I proceeded. He told me what a good ride he was; in fact he was extremely reliable and tried his best for his riders. I put this to her and she agreed, so my mind began to think maybe we are talking 'physical'; after all, it was a chiropractor that had passed my details on. I suggested that I 'body-scan' him, which I do by working from the mouth and all the way back. Some animals just 'stand quietly' as I point out what I can see, whereas others interrupt me all the way through and even ask me to scratch their belly, or tell me not to look 'under there'! This does sound impossible, as does a lot of what I do, but if I can clearly see a picture in my mind, then why can't I try to zoom in and study it closer? I went over this lad and, to be honest, there was really nothing to be found and told the owner that I wasn't being shown any problems. She said that made sense as the chiropractor had been on the yard to treat another horse, but had quickly checked Hugo to eliminate any pain issues. She had found nothing so then had suggested me.

I was getting nowhere, and she was still upset, so I decided to cut to the chase as she was clearly not enjoying this, and neither was I. I seemed to have a horse that was a good ride and physically sound and that chatted to me like a happy horse, so I decided to put it to her straight, "What direction do you want me to go in?" With that she hastily said, "Ask him what he has done to me!" "Okay," I said a bit hesitantly, and did just that. "Err, nothing," was his seemingly innocent reply. "Yes he did! He bit me, ask him why?" "Oh, that! I didn't mean to," said Hugo. "Well, it didn't seem like that to me. He has bitten me on my stomach and this is not the first time either!"

I could now see why she was upset and anxious; I would have been the same. If anyone else has experienced a serious horse bite you will know how painful and upsetting this can be. I told her I now understood her anger, however the horse didn't come across as the aggressive type but I would try to find out why.

He showed me someone putting their hand up to his mouth as his head was over the stable door. As soon as I told her she said, "That was it; that was the last time he did it!" "Were you trying to give him a titbit or something over the door?" I asked. "No," she replied, "I was trying to take his headcollar off." "Okay," I said, "but do you ever feed him titbits at the door?" "Very occasionally, but not often as he is a bit of a greedy horse."

I now had an inkling what was behind this, so decided to move on and ask about this latest misdemeanour. He then showed me a very calm picture of someone gathering up loose hay from the corner where his food manger was and bringing it across the stable to make a neat pile. I asked her if that picture made any sense and she said, "Yes, it was as I was moving the hay he grabbed my stomach." So I asked him, "Why did you bite her?" "I didn't mean to," Hugo replied, "I just thought she was going to take it away again!"

I asked her if sometimes whilst he was eating his food, did they take hay away from his stable? Yes and no was the answer. They would bring new hay into the stable, but if the pile of hay collected was big enough, sometimes they would then take some of the new hay back out of the stable with them. Now this was making sense. Imagine if your favourite food was chips, and someone everyday would bring you your plate of chips, then for whatever reason, remove some of them again on the way out, whilst you were finishing your starter. That would seem rather unfair, after all, you had been looking forward to those chips, and if you were greedy, like Hugo, you probably would have got rather annoyed at trying to eat one course whilst defending your second.

This turned out to be exactly what they were doing, and just as she stood up with the arm full of hay, he lunged to grab some and got her stomach instead. To be honest, no horse should snatch or bite, but unfortunately some do. This often stems from being a youngster when being bolder often meant you got more, very similar to being in the wild. He assured us that he had not meant to do it on either occasion and was extremely sorry indeed, and I truly thought he meant it.

Now we knew, I suggested that she never tries to take his headcollar off over the door so he cannot mistake her fingers on the way up. As for feed times, make sure that his feed is in his manger, the hay is cleared and piled to the right amount, and then put him in the stable and leave him to eat in peace.

By the end of the call, she was much calmer as the shock had worn off and the logic of the situation had taken over. She agreed that she now understood what the problem was, and that he had *not* been 'attacking her'; he was just being covetous of his food. She thought she would be able to cope with him now she had heard his side of the story. Although, she did admit, she would struggle to trust him for a while.

She said he was such a star in every other way and that she had felt in her own heart he wasn't really nasty but she was upset nevertheless. At least she knew now it was an unfortunate chink in his otherwise pretty perfect armour.

I didn't get an update personally from this owner, but about six months later, another person booked me from the same yard and assured me that there had been no more incidents and that Hugo's owner had 'got over it' and things were back to normal

*****

In the Bank

Although lots of people come to me because they simply want to hear what their animal wants to say, the majority are looking for solutions. Celia Baker, the manager of the Riding for the Disabled centre at Holme Lacey Hereford, also featured in my *Animal Insight* book about a pony called Toffee. It was a very interesting case and although we found out the problem, the result wasn't exactly what she would have hoped for. Although a horse may seem suited to their job there, in Celia's mind the welfare and happiness is paramount for the horses in her care.

The next 'patient' was called Murphy, a really good stamp of a horse who had been with the RDA for just over a year. He was dark bay with a white blaze, well built but athletic with it. He had been working well and doing all that they asked, which consisted mostly of being led round with the disabled children on board.

Celia, having run the centre for twenty plus years knew the signs when a horse had become bored and Murphy's time had come. Some horses are in the RDA for a huge part of their life and it suits them well, but some start to 'switch off' and, again, that varies from animal to animal.

Celia thought long and hard and decided to send him back to the dealer's yard he was brought from as they would surely find him a good home again. It was a sad day for the centre as Murphy was a genuine and easy horse and would always be remembered fondly.

That, basically, should have been the end of the story but no, things were really not going to plan. So once again, Celia decided to phone me and see if I, 'The Witch' (which coming from most people I would find rather unacceptable but it is her term of affection for me), could have a talk to him and find out what on earth was wrong?

As usual, Celia needed help very quickly so I didn't go down the photo route, I just got his description and age. Murphy was at this point still at the dealers yard but I was assured by Celia that she could pass on the information as she knew the dealer very well, and she was approachable. (I know dealers have a bad name and, to be honest, sadly, the majority deserve it but there are also some very good ones too. So just ask around and the ones with the good reputation will do their best to keep it that way.)

Murphy started off telling me how lovely he was but he really didn't want to go back.

"Go back where?" I enquired.

"To my previous home," he answered. Now I was totally confused. He was presently unhappy at the dealer's yard but he had certainly not been at Celia's so this didn't make sense. I asked him to be clearer and it transpired we were talking about the previous home who had originally sold him to this dealer. Celia knew his background and said that he had been a hunting horse, but didn't realise there had been a problem as such. Murphy explained that he didn't want to hunt again, as he had taught a beginner to hunt and it was not the most comfortable of tasks!

They had been kind to him but sometimes novice riders don't learn many riding skills before the hunting field, so the ride can turn into a lot of 'mouth pulling' and uncomfortable 'back thudding' when landing over jumps. This would make sense to us as to why an animal would rather not want to repeat the process. More importantly though, Murphy was keen to point out that he had been good enough and patient enough to put up with all this.

Upsettingly though, was that when his owner had achieved 'adequate' riding skills they had then sold him for a more up-market version! So, in his mind he felt totally let down, rather like someone practicing a starring role for a film and when it came to a public viewing being replaced by someone more glamorous! Celia knew that is why he had been 'traded in' and said she could understand that so I asked Murphy to show me how he was behaving presently.

Watching the pictures he was giving me, you would have never believed this horse had been surrounded by disabled children less than a week ago; as he was now barging and throwing his weight around; so in the end, the dealer had phoned Celia saying,

"What on earth has happened to Murphy? He is not the same horse we sold you a year ago!" Obviously, Celia was dismayed and said they had had no problems like that and then got the full story from her.

Although Murphy had been good to ride and even done some jumping with them, on the ground he was like an obnoxious teenager. A lady from a large BHS (British Horse Society) equestrian centre had been to see him. This BHS Centre was for students sitting their exams and she wanted to buy a capable horse for them to ride.

When she rode him he was good, not as good as he could have been but passable nevertheless, however, his manners were appalling. Unperturbed, she thought with work he would probably settle down and decided the next step was to arrange to have him vetted.

The vet went out a few days later and every time he tried to listen to Murphy's heart, or try to physically examine him, Murphy would be so stroppy that he was really starting to undo his sale. The owner wanted him to have a blood test done for this vetting but, as much as this vet tried, he could not get near enough to his neck to get a vein for the blood. This was so out-of-character for him, but the vets at the RDA could do anything with him. The vetting was stopped; the potential buyer was disappointed so she withdrew her interest.

Murphy showed me clearly what he had done, but, bizarrely, he was not talking to me in a stroppy way. Celia said that she understood that if he didn't want to go back to his old home that was fair enough. The problem was, if he didn't sort himself out he might have to go to the horse market and then where would he land up? I passed this all on and explained that actually he had just missed the opportunity of a fabulous home, so what did he want to do? His words,

"I just want to have fun!"

"Absolutely," we agreed.

"Don't we all? I replied. "This is why Celia has been kind enough to let you go, as she knew you were getting so bored." I then said, "So, Murphy, if we could find you a good home full of fun and interest, would you settle down and behave yourself?"

"Well, yes, but...," he replied, "I really would like to go back to the RDA and Celia could sell me from there!" Celia readily agreed and said the situation was embarrassing enough already. Also maybe there would be a chance she would contact the lady that was interested in him, if he agreed, to think about his actions. I put this to him, I thought it was a fair deal and he agreed and I asked for a bonding key to remind him of this conversation. He offered,

"It's so you can have fun!" This was his choice so Celia could say that should any nice person come to try him.

I wished her all the best and hoped that he would keep his word. At the end of the day, he was a smashing horse and was un-enamoured with his present 'job', so, he could actually get what he really wanted.

Within a few weeks I was to meet up with Celia and several friends from our local horse community for a very sad occasion. I and so many others were lucky enough to be able to call Di our friend.

Diane Lee was such an experienced horsewomen, she had a great 'eye' for the 'right' horse and just took everything in her stride. She had taught such a diversity of people, but to talk to her you would never have guessed she had actually even worked for royalty! She did, on a few occasions, mention 'The Captain' but, typically of her, it was said in such an unassuming way, I didn't even twig who she meant until someone else happened to tell me!

How funny this is – I only found out whilst writing this story that when the RDA was opened in June 1991 by Princess Anne, Di was her assistant in attendance! Di was honest, caring and had knowledge and patience in abundance, both for horses and her friends alike.

Sadly, in 2009 she had succumbed to breast cancer after a very long and courageous battle. She had fought the same battle ten years earlier but this time, sadly she was to lose. A couple of years ago when I found out I could do this work, Di was included amongst the people who I gave free talks to their animals. I was so pleased that I had the opportunity to share an animal talk with her. Di had been so supportive when I was fighting my own cancer battle, and although she knew she was losing hers, we had some long chats and agreed that we were sure that there was more to life than just down here.

It was on this Friday at the church, packed with so many friends and colleagues of Di's, that I met up with Celia. It was one of those services where, although a desperately sad occasion, there were funny little anecdotes that made us all remember and smile. Someone even gave out pale blue badges with 'I knew Di Lee' on them, so fitting and the type of funny thing Di would have thought of to organise for someone else.

With the service over, we set off to the local pub, as you do. Whilst walking I happened to ask Celia how the Murphy case had panned out, and she laughed and said,

"Cross your fingers, he is on a week's trial, and it is up on Monday!"

"Wow!" I said,

"How did you manage that?" Celia explained that she did indeed manage to persuade the same lady to come and see him back at the RDA, as he had come 'home' and become a perfect gentleman again. The lady came, tacked him up, rode him and handled him and not an ounce of barginess was to be seen. Celia said she had forgotten how many times in her head she had repeated, 'It's so you can have fun!'

Agreements were reached that they would have Murphy on a week's trial, see how he behaved and if he was good he would be vetted, and the cheque she left with Celia could be banked. Celia again said to me to cross my fingers as he had a big competition the next day (Saturday) – so here was hoping. I said I would ask my guides to help, wished her all the best and asked her to let me know the outcome.

The buyer phoned Monday evening to tell Celia she could bank the cheque with pleasure as he was an absolute star at the competition and was such a lovely sweet horse too! Celia phoned me to let me know the result, and what a result! The RDA got their money to buy another horse and, most of all, Murphy got what he wanted: Fun!

I sent this story to Celia (I always do if real identities are used) and I was delighted to hear that Murphy is adored and has turned out to be the horse that the students all love. He is so good that when given a choice the students choose him as their mount to sit their advanced exams!

This just goes to show how their thought process can be affected by memories, and being able to talk to these animals really can find out why they are acting as they are. With this horse, like others before him, it just took a conversation to explain to him, just like you would a person, to put the record straight, and what a difference it makes. (I am still amazed myself when animals change, and I will continue trying to make it happen. It is my job to give them a voice and an ear to listen, after all we sometimes need a shoulder to cry on or someone to defend our corner for us too.)

As Murphy had done his bit to teach someone on a beginner's level with all the 'unfortunates' that can go with that, how lovely that he is now appreciated for his skills at the higher level.

I will share something with you here that happened well after Murphy had been sold. By this time I had started on my *Celebrity Pet Talking* book and found that the only way I was going to find well known people was to be bold and ask, and keep asking. I must say it worked – and the book is proof of that itself.

As Bob is the horse dentist for the Hereford RDA, both he and I received a very posh invite – the Princess Royal, Princess Anne, was going to be visiting the centre and we were asked if we would like to attend the 'do'. How lovely to be asked and, of course, we would attend and it would be a great occasion to look forward to.

A couple of hours before we were due to leave to travel to Hereford I suddenly remembered having read somewhere that apparently Princess Anne had used an animal psychic, and they had discovered one of her horses had a problem with a bone in its neck. This was maybe not true, but it might have been so an idea sprung into my head, what if...

I sat at my computer and quickly composed a letter to be included in the unsealed envelope containing a copy of my *Animal Insight* book. I put it in my handbag and we arrived on time and stood where we were all told and waited, and waited. She had been held up at the previous place and was now about an hour behind schedule.

Princess Anne duly arrived and greeted the guests of honour who were being thanked for their years of hard work and help. She went and stood on the podium and started to give a speech. Bob urged me to go and give my envelope to one of her body guards. I approached one and he said he couldn't take it but to go over to another man and give it to him. It was ridiculous – I was so nervous as if I was doing something wrong. Eventually with more cajoling from Bob I sneaked up to the gentleman and asked if he could pass the book and letter on. He asked if the book had been written by me and I assured him it had. He smiled, took it and minutes later the Princess Royal finished her speech and left.

Sadly, in spite of my efforts, nothing came of it although I am the proud owner of an official letter from Buckingham Palace thanking me anyway. The closest I did get to in my *Celebrity Pet Talking* book was… chatting to a dog that her mother, The Queen, had actually bred and given to someone who I chatted to from spirit!

Now back to stories written by the owners themselves…

A small boy with a huge personality...

Claire, Pete and their cat Chip

In October 2014, our beloved Chip came into our lives and changed it forever.

We have a very busy household already with four Springer Spaniels and our cat Buddy but there was still something missing, and then along came Chip. He was a black Siamese-cross, a tiny little thing with long gangly legs and big bat like ears, but he was adorable!

For a small kitten he certainly had a big set of lungs on him, complete with the bossiest and loudest meow I have ever heard! I was a bit worried introducing him to our dogs but I needn't have worried, Chip was fearless – the poor dogs didn't know what to do! Buddy, our other cat, is very laid back and slept most of the day, but not so much when Chip was around - he was like a naughty, annoying little brother.

There wasn't a dull moment with Chip. My boyfriend, Pete even had to climb a tree to rescue him as he climbed so high he couldn't come down! Chip had a very special bond with Pete; he would literally jump into his arms when he saw him and follow him around the garden – a right daddy's boy.

The morning of Friday the 26th of June is a day we will never forget

I got up and set off to work in the car as usual. I pulled out of our road and into the dual carriageway, as I did I saw something on the side of the road, "Oh no another badger," I thought, but as I drove closer I saw that it was jet black. My heart sank to the pit of my stomach. I drove as slow as I could to see, but I couldn't get a good view – I had to turn back. At this point I was an emotional wreck, frantically trying to call Pete but he didn't answer. I tried to keep calm but I knew deep down it was Chip. I drove back home to get Pete as I couldn't bear to go back by myself. We both got in his car and pulled up beside him. It was Chip. I've never cried with such heartache in my life, I couldn't believe this was happening.

We had him cremated – he was only ten months old. Pete was devastated; I've never seen him cry like that before. The days after were awful; we both just moped around the house, sometimes bursting into tears without warning. As much as our house is busy with all the dogs and Buddy – it seemed so empty without our Chippy.

We felt sadness, anger and guilt. We just felt so cheated and had so many questions:

Why was he so near the main road?

Did he suffer? What happened?

That's when I found Jackie.

I've never heard of an animal psychic before and was quite sceptical, but after reading rave reviews online and ordering several of Jackie's books we arranged a reading via telephone. We put Jackie on loud-speaker so both of us could listen. We were both quite nervous but Jackie was so nice and put us at ease straightaway. She explained that it would be like a three-way-conversation and to jot down anything that doesn't make sense to us as it might come to light later on.

"Chip describes himself as bold and full of life. Would you say that's right?" "That's our Chip!" we chimed.

"Was it a accident? About 100 yards away from your house?" We agreed, Jackie got the distance 100% accurate.

"He was hit by a car wasn't he?" We agreed again and I started to get upset.

Jackie apologised and said this is Chip's description of it as, "Bang, dead, gone. He didn't feel any pain. It was very sudden."

It gave us such comfort knowing that he didn't feel any pain, as the biggest upset for me was not knowing if he suffered.

"Does somebody kiss a picture of Chip on the phone?" she asked. "I did." Pete said. "I've got him as my screensaver on my mobile and kissed it the other day." I had no idea Pete did this.

"Chip says please don't be sad, you're both such lovely people. I loved being outdoors – I would have hated being cooped in all the time." This was also comforting to hear, as we felt guilty thinking that if we had kept him in more maybe this accident wouldn't have happened.

"Little white dove? Chip just said little white dove?" We had no idea what that meant but Jackie suggested we jotted it down anyway.

"He just said... chipmunk? Does that mean anything?" Chipmunk was his nickname we told her. Chip had so many nicknames and Chipmunk was one of mine I gave him. I couldn't believe it; it felt like we were talking to Chip. It was truly amazing.

"Claire, do you have a Nan (Grandmother) who has passed who you were close to?" Jackie asked. I hadn't, but Pete had. He was incredibly close to his Nan as a child but she sadly passed with breast cancer. "Chip wants to tell you that whenever you think of your Nan, that's her whispering in your ear." Pete was crying at this point, it was just so much more personal than we were expecting.

Jackie asked if we had any questions for Chip. "Why was he so far up the road?" we asked. "Get off my patch, get off my patch," he kept saying the same thing over and over. Jackie explained that it seemed he was on another cat's territory and got scared and ran into the main road.

There was so much more Jackie said to us that only we would know. It was truly a wonderful experience! After the reading, we both sat there and cried-both sad and happy tears.

Later on that evening Pete went to work (he's a pest control officer and uses birds of prey to do so.) We are due to get married in September 2016 and had been struggling to choose a song for our first dance. I was on the computer looking up different songs old and new. Then, for some reason the song *Power of Love* by Huey Lewis came into my head so I started playing it. I must have heard that song a hundred times before but now the lyrics, 'change a hawk to a little white dove' stuck out like a sore thumb. Chip's dad works with hawks and those words about a little white dove from the reading! I couldn't believe it. I believe in my heart that it was a message from chip deciding for us. I called Pete instantly and he agreed, so we're having it as our wedding song.

We cannot thank Jackie enough for our reading. The heartache will always be there but Jackie has given us so much comfort and has eased the pain immensely.

Knowing that our Chippy is still alive and well in the spirit world is a fantastic feeling.

Thank you. Thank you for sharing your amazing gift.

We love you Chip! Forever and always. Xxx

*****

A complete misunderstanding...

Diane and her dog Jess

I saw Jess on a dog rescue website, she was actually called Jill then. She was a lovely girl with beautiful, but very sad, eyes. When my husband, Mark, came home, I showed him this little Collie I had been drawn to and said that I thought she could be our next dog. We had actually just had to have two of our three dogs put to sleep and Ava, now our only dog, was clearly upset too.

The description of Jess said that she was a very shy girl who lacked confidence as she had been through a lot and hadn't had a very good start in life. It said that she was aged about seven months and seemed to get on with other dogs. I contacted the rescue and arranged to go to see her with Mark later on that day. We were told that she had lived on a farm but was not thought to be good enough to work and so the farmer had taken her to the vets to be put to sleep. The vet took her and got in touch with the rescue to see if they would try and find her a home. They agreed and we were now going to see this poor innocent dog.

When we got to the kennels, Jess was brought out to us by one of the staff. She was very thin, her ribs were visible through her dull and lifeless coat. She was a very shy and frightened looking Collie but still her eyes said so much. We took her for a little walk and talked to her but she was just so scared and wary of us. We thought it would be difficult but we just knew we had to look after her. The following day we took our daughter, Becci, to meet her; she seemed a little better in herself and got on well with Ava and so we filled in the paperwork, paid our donation and took her home. She was terrified getting in the van but was fine on the journey home and she now became our 'Jess'.

This was Jess's second chance to have a happy life. She lacked confidence and was very timid but settled in quite well. She was very scared of sudden noise and we had to be really careful around her but that was fine, we didn't mind. It was now up to us to help her to gain our trust. She watched Ava a lot and started to copy her sometimes but she didn't play at all nor act like a puppy. It really was as if she didn't know how to.

All was well until after about six weeks. I was at work and chatting on the phone with my daughter Becci who was at home. We were just talking away when suddenly my daughter screamed down the phone that Jess was attacking Ava. As soon as I heard that I rushed home. Becci had managed to get Jess off Ava but Ava was distressed and bleeding from her side where Jess had bitten her. We quickly took Ava to the vets.

We were absolutely devastated; Jess had never before shown any signs of aggression. It was decided that she would not be able to remain with us, as it wasn't fair to Ava as she was so tiny compared to Jess, we felt we could not take any chances. The problem was, that Mark was starting to bond with Jess and her with him and I could see that he didn't want to send her back to the kennels, even though they had been kind to her there. We considered the options and decided that if she had to go anywhere, we would like her to go to Battersea Dogs Home. We had seen it on the TV programmes with Paul O'Grady and knew they would look after her and help her. It would be the best possible chance for her due to her lack of confidence, and now this latest behavioural issue, as they do a lot of dog rehabilitation work. The following day I spoke to a lovely man at Battersea who had said what we all thought, that it was most likely that Ava and Jess had fallen out over a toy or bone or something. He agreed that we could take Jess down to them at the weekend – we are about three to four hours away from there. It was the least we could do for this poor little girl at least she could perhaps have another chance to be happy with someone who maybe didn't have another dog.

I already had an appointment booked with Jackie for a reading with my two dogs who had passed over a few weeks previously, as I was struggling to cope with losing them. The appointment had been arranged for the night after the incident with Ava and Jess but I was so upset about it I had to postpone the appointment. Jackie was very sweet when I explained what had happened and she sent Ava some healing and I said I would ring her to re-arrange the reading.

Ava was healing well and getting back to her usual lively self, thank goodness. We still loved Jess and all of us, including Becci, did not want to give up on her but we didn't know what to do because of Ava. We didn't want to risk it happening again or perhaps worse. Suddenly I had a thought... perhaps Jackie could help us with this heart-wrenching situation. I rang Jackie and I told her that we were now thinking about keeping Jess and could she help. She thought she could (although expressed that she couldn't make any promises) and so the photos were sent to her of both dogs and a chat with Jess was arranged for that evening.

Becci was with me for the call. Jackie tuned in with Jess straight away and first asked Jess to tell her a little about herself. The first thing that Jess said was that she was not a nasty dog but was easily startled. Jackie asked if Ava was a yappy dog and we confirmed that she is a very yappy dog. Jackie said that she got the feeling that Ava had been yapping just before the incident with Jess. We hadn't even thought about it but Becci immediately said that she had been yapping just before she let them out into the garden when the attack took place. Jackie said that she thought Jess had reacted out of fright. This now made sense to us as she had shown no sign of aggression until this. Jackie said that she thought Ava was trying to get Jess to play and be as happy as she was. Jess told Jackie that she didn't understand what was going on – again this made sense as she had never tried to play or act like a puppy since we got her. She told Jackie that she would be a loyal dog. Jackie said that she thought that Jess was suddenly going to realise that she could be silly and act like a puppy as she had never had the chance to be a carefree puppy nor did she know how to act like one.

Jackie then asked if Jess was noise reactive and she was, very much – if you just coughed or sneezed she'd jump up and run behind the settee or go to her bed. She said that Jess was not completely relaxed yet and this was reflected in her behaviour around the house. Jess then told Jackie that she liked Ava and also added that Ava had a fat little belly, which was very true! Jackie then went on to say that she didn't feel that Jess wanted to be dominant and that is true; she had never shown any sign of wanting to be top dog in the house.

Jess then told Jackie that she was scared of getting in the way, just as we had thought. She would always make sure that she could see us and would walk backwards to move for us. Jackie assured Jess that she wasn't in the way and if she did over step the mark we would tell her BUT whatever she does she cannot attack Ava. Even though Ava is guilty of barking, and sometimes close to her face at that, it is not meant aggressively so Jess must walk away and not retaliate. Jackie told her that the house was for sharing and she was not in the way.

Jackie then said that Jess would benefit from some training, the man I spoke to at Battersea had said the same. As Jess was so nervous, Jackie told her that it didn't matter if she got things wrong and that no one would shout at her. She thought Jess was a focused dog and could count. We knew she was smart too.

Jess told Jackie again that she was not nasty. Jackie then told her that we would trust her word on that. She told Jackie that she could make bonds – she was certainly doing so now with Mark. Jackie said to build on that bond to gain her trust. Jess said that she wanted Mark to train her, not a stranger like an animal behaviourist. Jackie told Jess that she would have a lovely life with us but again pointed out that she was not to bite Ava or any other dog and if she ever did, sadly things would be very different. She again told her not to retaliate but to just run away.

Jackie had a few words about her toilet habits, which we were finding difficult, as she had been used to being outside all of the time and so never knew to go outside. Jackie told her that if she could see the sky (she quickly checked if we did not have a conservatory!) then she could wee or poo. This has worked very well with only with the odd little accident since.

Jess was scared when we tried to stroke her. She would only let us stroke her head, but Jackie explained to her that we were not going to hurt her and if we touched her, it was just to give her some love and attention. She had major trust issues due to being mistreated by the farmer.

Jackie then asked if our little terrier Ava lay on her back with her legs in the air? It was strange but she does and had been earlier on that evening and Becci was fussing and cuddling her and Jess was watching so interested as if to say, I wish I could be like that. Then Jess said, "Tell Ava I'm sorry" How sweet. Jess said that Ava had not changed towards her since it had happened and that was true, Ava acted like the incident had never happened, which was surprising after what she had been through.

Jackie then asked if there was anything else and I just asked Jackie if she thought that it would happen again, as we needed to know that Ava was safe. Jackie said that she didn't think that it would (but expressed that was only her opinion and feeling about this) and that it was just that Ava was trying to get Jess to play and Jess didn't understand what was going on. Jackie then told Jess to let go of the past and forget about her previous life and everything would be fine. She told us just to explain everything to Jess like you would a child. Jackie finished the chat with Jess by saying to her that she could play and said hopefully, she would realise that she could be a puppy.

We are so very grateful to Jackie for giving us the chance to hear Jess's side of things and explain exactly what had happened with the girls that day. It all made sense and especially to Becci who was there at the time to confirm the facts. If it had not been for Jackie we would never have known what happened. It gave us the confidence to again believe in our new little girl knowing it was not her intent to hurt Ava. We thought she deserved another chance and we are so pleased that we gave it to her.

It's been just over six months now and Ava and Jess get on so well together, they have their little moments as Ava is a typical terrier but Jess is learning from Ava all the time. She is still a little shy but so much more confident than when we first met her. She loves to play especially play fighting with Ava. She plays with toys, chews bones and runs around just like a little (maybe big) puppy now. She loves her walks with Mark and is lovely when meeting any dogs; she even lies down as if to say, "I'm friendly." She has learned some tricks and can now shake a paw and give kisses on cue! It's amazing how she has come on so well. She now looks happy and content, she has put weight on and her coat is so lovely and shiny. As a rescue dog, who had been through so much, she did not understand how family life was. She didn't know that people would only love and care for her and not abuse her. She is now trusting us and understanding our love for her.

We are truly grateful to Jackie for giving Jess the chance to tell us how she felt – it has helped so much.

She is now a precious member of our family and a great friend to Ava. We know that it was the right decision to keep her and it would have been awful for all of us to give up on her. Rescue dogs go through so much, whatever their reason for being where they are, and deserve a chance to explain how they feel. We thank Jackie so much for her help. I am sure that Jess does too and of course, not forgetting Ava who now has a wonderful dog friend once again.

*****

A big and beautiful Angel...

Arwel and his dog Sky

Sky was a beautiful, gentle St Bernard. She had such a big personality, the type I had never experienced with any other dog before. She epitomised the term most commonly used to describe this breed 'Gentle Giants'.

She first came into my life at three months old and I made a very long journey to meet her. What made Sky unusual was that she was termed a mismark due to the fact that she did not have the full mask that St Bernard's normally have around their eyes. Instead, she had one brown eye and one white eye; it was obvious she was born to be different!

I bonded very quickly with Sky; we became inseparable. It was hard even to go away for a few weeks holiday without her being around. I am convinced she thought she was more human than dog, and preferred the attention of passers-by rather than the dog they may have had with them. Being an unusual dog, a 30 minute walk would quickly be an hour due to the attention she received from passers-by. Sky soon became accustomed to this attention and considered it 'the norm', and as a young puppy she would bark and cry at people who would walk past her without paying attention and fussing her!

Sky enjoyed any attention even if it was going to the vets! Whilst I would see other dogs pulling away from the vets, Sky would recognise the building on our walk and pull to go in. One morning when we walked in, the secretary had just organised the counter and tidied up and placed the leaflets in their positions. Upon hearing her name, Sky enthusiastically jumped up at the counter sending the leaflets flying everywhere – everyone knew when Sky arrived!

I was devastated in April that, at only six-years-old, Sky was diagnosed in the latter stages of Lymphoma. She had stopped eating and was not herself. Even though she was given only a few months to live although being treated with chemotherapy, Sky's strong will shone through and she lasted until December of the same year.

I remember a conversation a week before her passing whilst out on a walk. Sky was obsessed with squirrels but, being slow and big, she could never get near them. One day she found a squirrel who had unfortunately passed away and looked at him, had a sniff, and I told her, "Your life purpose/ambition is now complete my friend."

It was December the 15th and the hardest day of my life. She had given up – she had swollen up and her back legs had given upon her. It was hard when it was time to send her to the other side and I could not stop crying. At one point I was on the verge of walking out of the consultation room, but I made a promise to Sky at three months old that I would be there for her forever. When the time came, she took one last breath and went whilst I kissed the top of her head.

I found Jackie online, and being spiritual myself, I knew that a reading would afford me closure as I had a few questions unanswered. As soon as Jackie started her reading, it was obvious that it was Sky coming through. Jackie gave me lots of confirmation, including Sky's passion of being tickled behind the ear and the cat who used to visit that Sky was jealous I was feeding. The fact that I used to joke that should Sky had ever had puppies, she would get jealous of having to share my attention, to name only a few confirmations, that alone would fill a chapter in itself. I was told so much, and things that only Sky and I would know.

My questions involved the day of her passing, even though she was ill, it came all of a sudden, and I wanted to know if Sky was ready to go and how she felt about her passing. Sky described this day to Jackie as a bittersweet day. She told Jackie she loved the fact that I had taken her for a final walk and fed her special treats. These were a chocolate bar and a mince pie, as she had always wanted to eat some and I did it as a final gift to Sky. She wanted me to know that her passing was made more comfortable with me kissing her head as she left this Earth. Sky confirmed that it was her time to go and that she would still be around me.

I felt her presence on Christmas day and Jackie also confirmed this. The reading gave me closure and assurance that Sky lives on and will be around me. Daily, I still find it hard thinking about Sky, but I have a lot of comfort from the reading and know I will see her again one day.

*****

A little bird with a huge heart...

Diane and her Song Thrush Flo

In late May 2014 I was on my way home from work when I saw a young bird in the middle of the road in the village of Flers in Picardy, Northern France. She was squawking and having a right song and dance, trying to fly, but she was a fledgling Song Thrush so finding it impossible. I was worried that she was drawing attention from the local cats, plus a car may easily have run her over, so I moved her off the road to a nearby wall. I then drove off but could not settle so I went back only to find her still there with her mother nowhere in sight. I decided to scoop her up and take her home, as we had rescued a ring collar dove in the past and released her back into the wild. I got home and tried to feed her, but found it very difficult, so decided to return her. The same thing happened and so I finally brought her back home. Obviously I would have to persist with feeding her, so cat food it was for the time being. The dove's diet had been easier as she was mainly vegetarian.

We named her Flo, having found her in Flers, although she could have been Fred; in time we realised we had given her the correct name! As we have a number of cats keeping her was going to be a challenge, so I placed her where she could be free to walk around in our office bathroom. In time she loved to hop between the yucca plant and the shelf, and then the bathroom sink. She loved dancing on the taps.

I read on the Internet that their natural food was the earthworm. Well there I was digging for worms, being a vegetarian myself this was difficult, plus she was still far too young to know what to do with them. I also had a pang of guilt offering her these live creatures. Locally you can buy worms in a plastic container, these are for sale for the fishermen, but I found opening it to be quite repulsive. I would try to feed her in a cage on the lawn but most of the worms, if not all, managed to get away into the ground. I was secretly happy to see them liberated but knew that there had to be a better solution. We also tried wild berries which Flo loved; being early summer these where not always in abundance so we regularly defrosted frozen berries.

We found the solution to her diet with dried mealworms. In time I got used to them, but at first I could not look at the packet. We could not find them to buy locally so the good old Internet supplied them. Plus friends popping over to visit the UK would be asked to pop a bag of mealworms in their suitcases. Our friends know us well so this did not seem a strange request.

When we first rescued Flo we realised she had a bad eye. We thought in time it would heal, but it never did. Maybe her mother knew she was not 100% and, as always, it is survival of the fittest in the animal kingdom. She would cock her head to one side when trying to find her food, a really quaint movement. We would talk to her and say how beautiful she was and she seemed to look at us as if understanding what we were saying.

We sourced a small cage so she could go onto our lawn which the cats loved. We invented a sort of tepee so the cats could not claw at her much to their annoyance. She loved spreading her wings in the sunshine; it was a joy to witness. One other thing we loved watching was her having a bath. She would get into it and stand and just spin her wings into the water with her head ducked in as well, and then she was like a helicopter as she shook her wings to dry. She went in several times just to make sure she was clean all over and then it was time to bask in the sunshine to dry her wings. We adored watching her grow into an adult bird.

Inside her bathroom she loved to fly onto our shoulders and also be fed whilst on our fingers; she was so tame from the beginning and so trusting. You could walk around the house and she would not attempt to fly off; but if she did she was soon back onto you, either on your head or back onto your hand. She thrived on attention.

Soon after I rescued her we had to have friends look after her, as we were both out working so much and she needed regular food and fresh water. We were still feeding her cat food at that stage. She had several temporary homes and touched the hearts of all our friends who all said how tame and friendly she was. Everyone said Flo was exceptional and how she was a very special bird.

Our plan was always to release her, but she was so vulnerable with her poor eyesight. With her being a wild bird, it was a tricky one, as you are not supposed to keep them. After a couple of months we did try to release her, taking her to a friend's garden, but all she did was go from one tree to another, with us transporting her whilst she groomed herself! Our hearts were in our mouths I must say, but we were relieved to see she was not ready to go.

In time we purchased a much larger cage and we built an aviary about three metres long so then she could fly. The plan was that she would be outdoors most of the time, even during the night. She loved this as we had made many perches, so she could fly and hop all over her new dwelling.

In July we had planned a holiday to Brittany staying in a gîte. We were not averse in taking our cats away with us when they were either kittens or were sick and needed extra care, so naturally Flo came with us. The journey was quite interesting too as we had to go through many toll booths and wondered what the police would have said if they had seen Flo, being a wild bird. We quickly popped a towel over her cage to hide the evidence! We checked to see if the gîte allowed animals and indeed they did. I am not sure the owner expected a Song Thrush though. We assured her Flo would be kept in her cage in the house but would also like to take it outside in it onto the lawn or on the patio table. I must say, the owner's wee Jack Russell was very curious about Flo but she was not fazed in the slightest.

We would go off to the beach leaving Flo outside on the table in the shade, but I must say we were always relieved to see her safe in her cage on our return. One of her characteristics, which we loved, was that when she was asleep, she would rest on just one leg with her head tucked into her feathers. We had never witnessed this until our trip to Brittany.

On one occasion Flo could have found freedom in her early years as I accidentally left a door open on her cage. I subsequently went out shopping and on my return saw her cage was empty. I was then in panic mode, running all over the garden calling her name, and when I looked back at the house, there she was on our dining room roof just sitting there looking at me wondering what all the fuss was about! Flo was instantly recognisable, being the fattest Song Thrush ever, and often she reminded us of a Partridge. I could get access to the roof via our bedroom so off I ran as she seemed quite happy to be just sit there. When she saw me on the roof she moved away getting further beyond my reach, however with one leap across the roof I managed to grab her, much to her irritation, but I was much happier. I am not sure what our neighbours would have thought if they had seen me flying across the roof!

Flo stayed outside all through the winter of 2014. We had put a wooden box high up in the cage for her, and blocked off one side of the cage where the easterly winds were prevalent. It made our hearts sing when we saw her in there one early evening. We had snow that year and it was a joy to see her pushing up the snow into the air as she pecked the ground.

Coming into the spring of 2015, I was doing my daily routine of going to feed her, with her favourite meal of mealworms that we softened with warm water. She was also keen on having a small piece of granary bread each day too. It was earlier than normal and the birds were in full song. On reaching her cage I heard her sing; she was fluttering her wings, singing and almost in a trance. Her song just blew me away and I was mesmerised. So magical was the moment, I stayed there transfixed. They say Song Thrushes have a huge range of songs and I was so privileged to witness one of them.

We then noticed her start to collect twigs and grass over the next few days, by her natural instinct, Flo was starting to build a nest in the wooden box we had placed inside for her. We gathered more dried grass for her, which she took straightaway into her new abode; again it was just an incredible moment. She created a wonderful nest and was, of course, showing all the natural instincts a wild bird would have.

We again felt uneasy that sadly Flo would miss out on meeting a mate. It was natural she should be free, but would she be safe? Could she survive? We had many discussions with our friends and a wild animal care charity about what was best for her. Everyone said how vulnerable she was and would have to be protected, but in our hearts we wanted her to be free too.

In the summer I was out feeding Flo when I saw this perfectly shaped pale blue egg. She was a bit bemused and did not know what to do with it; it was just lying there on the bottom of her cage. This also was another sign that she was showing all the natural bird instincts and, of course, it lay unfertilised. Her singing in the morning got louder and longer as she tried to encourage a mate, and we did hear other Song Thrushes high in the trees near her. Every day we were finding eggs in different places in her aviary.

After much discussion we attempted to try and release her, as the dilemma of what we should do was haunting us. We put all of our cats inside and opened Flo's door gingerly. She got out, but seemed completely unaware of what was around her. As she got further and further away she continuously pecked the ground; we could not settle, so I collected her and popped her back into her aviary. This was proof she was going to have to be in this for life due to her vulnerability.

Several weeks passed and we had friends over to help us do some major gardening on a new house we had built next to where we lived, moving great tree trunks and shovelling earth. I had seen Flo in the morning but I was conscious of helping my friends with the day ahead.

Mid morning one of my friends said how she could hear Flo singing, as she could hear her voice; the beautiful sound of a Song Thrush. I thought nothing of it until my friend popped next door to see Flo only to find she was not in her cage. She came back with the news. I ran over to see if she was mistaken, but no Flo had found a gap in the cage, either on the ground where she had been digging, or at the top where the roof sat on the cage. I was frantic, calling her, trying to see where she was in the undergrowth but with no success. It was a nightmare and all my worst fears had happened. Full of guilt I punished myself for not looking after her properly, as I had not checked that her cage was closed for gaps. We searched and searched all day. What had started out to be a fun gardening day had turned sour.

That evening I could not rest and stayed outside looking for her. Suddenly one of the cats came into the garden with a bird just like Flo. I ran over and distracted our cat but could not find the bird. It had got away in the undergrowth.

Several days passed but there was no sign of Flo. We were beside ourselves. Maybe she had got away, maybe this is how it was supposed to be, but we felt empty inside. She was such an amazing bird and had made such a huge impact on our lives. We always saw her first thing in a morning and then last thing at night. Not just us, but everyone was sad but we held onto the possibility that she was still alive.

As I could not settle, I decided one morning, about three days after Flo had left, to clear away some bracken behind her old aviary near the apple trees. This is when I found her. There did not seem to be a mark on her and her feathers were not ruffled, she was just lying there. I knew it was our dear Flo because of her blind eye. I ran into the house full of tears with her. We buried her in a box in our garden along with all our lost pets over the years. We could not bear to see her aviary every day, so we removed that the same day.

It was so hard. We had admitted she was vulnerable and had decided to not release her when this happened; I could not get closure and I felt like we had let her down. We had been through everything together, and now this; at just a year old, just when she was becoming mature. Her loss devastated us. We missed her so much and it was the first time I had thought about contacting an animal spiritualist. I was not even sure if there was such a person, or if birds came into the category and whether they could communicate, but I knew if any bird could, Flo could. She was so smart.

I searched the Internet and found Jackie Weaver; the testimonials were proof enough that Jackie was genuine. I had never done this sort of thing before, so with trepidation, I sent an e-mail asking firstly if a bird could be included in this sort of communication, Jackie came back by return saying of course. I was already overwhelmed just thinking would it be possible. We have lost pets before, dearly loved as they all are, but for some reason I just needed closure with Flo. She was different and had really depended on us to keep her safe.

A couple of weeks passed. I had already sent Jackie just her name, how old she was when she died, and a photograph. Flo always showed us her good side; I suppose she was trying to see us with her good eye so it generally was just showing one eye. I did not mention to Jackie anything else.

We set a time and we Skyped each other via web cam. I was so nervous, not knowing what to expect, but the reading did more than Jackie will ever know.

Initially Jackie asked why is Flo showing her a musical score? She did not know that Flo was a Song Thrush and of course she had a massive range of songs. She asked, "What is this large column she keeps showing me?" This of course was the bathroom sink pedestal where she had spent so much of her time playing. Also, she asked, "Why is she cocking her head to one side?" I explained that this was so that she can see her food as she was actually blind in the other eye. She mentioned the mealworms and all sorts of things which no-one would have known.

The icing on the cake was when Jackie asked about the weather vane which had blown down. This had been a gift for our new house and we had had some high winds which just left East and West on the roof! Flo said we should buy a new one in memory of her.

On her passing Jackie asked Flo about what happened. Flo said she was flying when, all of sudden, she hit a tree and it was instantaneous. I had felt really guilty that it was one of our cats, but knowing this has really helped. It makes sense now as her feathers were not ruffled. Towards the end of the conversation Jackie asked if I would like to ask Flo anything, I blurted out 'Yes'. 'Did she feel we had let her down right at the end when we had not thoroughly re-checked her cage?' Her response was 'No'; it was her choice to leave, she was desperate to meet a new mate and it would only have got worse.

This has given us closure knowing she is well, and apparently Flo has been telling all her friends in her new life how she has witnessed human kindness. She knew too how beautiful she was, she was and always will be. She was gentle in spirit and just a joy to have in our lives, if only for a short time. We miss her but this reading has just brought such serenity, especially with all the other pets we have had and cared for during our lives. Thank you Jackie, your gift is priceless.

*****

Love that shines eternal...

Kirsty and her horse Cuddles

Ever since I was a little girl I have always been into horses. I started riding when I was around eight-years-old at my local riding stables, which was the same stables my mum, Susan, had also learnt to ride at many years ago. I fell in love with a horse called Bingo and used to get my mum to book him for me six weeks in advance so nobody else could have him for my lesson. He was a beautiful skewbald traditional cob and getting to know him is how I fell in love with cobs. One day a new horse called Whiskey arrived – he was blue and white and had the most stunning, long flowing thick mane and tail, and these beautiful blue eyes. I remember thinking back then, "When I'm older this is exactly how I want my horse to look."

As I got older, I started getting more involved helping out at the stables. I would spend my whole weekends down there; I loved every minute. For my mum, it was like going back in time. I relived her steps, as she had begun helping out there, then worked there and used to take the rides out. I know my mum's biggest regret was giving it up when she got married and had a family. Even if I do get married and have a family, I will keep my boy whatever.

Although when I became a teenager I ended up leaving to do 'teenage' things: hanging out with my friends etc. After a long break away from horses, my life was about to change for the better.

Three and a half years ago I was casually browsing the Internet looking at what different kinds of horses were for sale. I have to say, I had no intention of having one, although I had left the horsey world, it had clearly not left my heart. Whilst flicking through the adverts, a horse called Cuddles popped up and I thought, "What a cute name.' I clicked on to his pictures and description and knew I had to go and see him. Almost straight away I rang the people and made an appointment to see him that weekend. I told my parents, much to their surprise I might add, as, like I have mentioned, I had been away from horses for years and I didn't even own a pair of horse riding boots!

The weekend arrived; I was so excited, my parents came with me to see him. When I arrived and saw him in the stable he was windsucking on the door (a vice often created through boredom or nerves) and looked pretty scrawny. He was very nervous and the lady said he had been through a lot with his previous owners. When she brought him out of the stable I knew instantly he was the one for me; he was blue and white with the thickest, most gorgeous tail and mane I have ever seen. When I looked closer at his face I noticed he had half blue and half brown eyes, which is quite unusual. I couldn't believe it; I knew this was the horse I had dreamed of owning, from when I first saw Whiskey back at the riding stables when I was a little girl. My wish had come true.

My dad tried to talk me out of wanting him because of his problems. This would be my first horse and he was a little worried for me but my mum understood. I went with my heart and my gut; I paid the deposit for him there and then. I went home a very happy lady. As soon as it was Monday I rang the vets and booked him for a 5* vetting. I was telling the receptionist a little bit about him and she even tried to talk me out of having him too but, needless to say, of course I didn't listen! It was the day of the vetting, I was very nervous but he passed everything, I was so relieved. I paid the remaining balance and arranged for him to be delivered at the weekend.

I sorted out a place for his livery and when Saturday arrived, I was up bright and early making sure everything was perfect for his arrival. When I heard a horsebox coming round the corner I was so happy and excited, but he looked so scared and worried as if wondering where he was and what was happening. He needed such a lot of time and patience for him to come around and realise there was no need to be nervous of me. My patience paid off and once I started gaining his trust, everything was going in the right direction.

A month after I had owned him, my world fell apart, as my mum passed away from a long battle with cancer – it was such a devastating time and Cuddles was the one who helped me through. I can truly say, without him, I don't know how I would have coped. He's not just a horse to me, he's my healer, my fun, my world; he brought me happiness when I was in such a heartbroken state. I now know we were meant for each other; he was guided to me and I was guided to him. We were both broken and have fixed each other.

There's not a day goes by that I don't appreciate him. I never take him for granted, the loving feeling I get every time I see him is beyond words. I love him with all of my heart. We share such a special, magical, one-of-a-kind type of bond and everyday that bond gets stronger and stronger.

Two years ago Cuddles had a bad accident in the field – I left him absolutely fine on a Friday night and when I arrived the next morning I was devastated to find he could hardly walk on his hind legs; I called the vet immediately. He got sent to hospital for ten days, I was beside myself and I went to visit him everyday. One of the scans showed a hotspot on the right side of his back, so they started treatment injections and physio that went on for several months. Over time he gradually improved but, as he is a very playful horse in the field, it doesn't take much for him to show signs of being sore. Since his accident he gets uncomfortable from time to time but with regular chiropractor visits things are under control.

We have grown so much together and I have always wondered what had happened to him. I began researching animal communicators, I did a lot of research and looked into a lot of people, but the name that stood out for me was Jackie Weaver. I clicked on her website and started reading about her; when I found out about her awful battle with cancer too, I felt an instant connection towards her as I know what she, and her loved ones, had gone through. I knew Jackie was the one I wanted to do my reading for myself and Cuddles. I emailed straight away and when I got her reply, I thought, "What a lovely lady" and had an appointment booked for the following Friday.

The day had arrived and I was feeling a little nervous, but as soon as the phone rang and I answered, Jackie's voice made me feel at ease, she is very warm and friendly. One of the first things Jackie said was that Cuddles had told her that I don't need to worry about sitting on his back hard as it doesn't bother him! She said it sounded a bit of an odd statement and I was amazed and actually asked Jackie to repeat herself to double check I had heard correctly. I can now finally sit on my boy and relax without the worry of, 'Am I hurting him?' To know he is absolutely fine helps me so much. Jackie then talked about an accident he had and how he did it, I felt so relieved to finally know what had actually happened.

Cuddles described to Jackie as going out riding as his 'playtime', how adorable! For Cuddles to describe going out riding as his 'playtime' fits in with what I ask, and don't ask, of him: I don't ask him to take me out riding every day of the week, I don't ride him in the school, I don't make him go in a forced outline; I let him go in his own natural way, I don't ask him to compete. He is my pleasure horse and we hack out every now and then and we have so much fun. We even go on summer picnics, which Jackie mentioned, and Cuddles said he loves it. I don't try and fit in with what others do, or what others think I should do, I do my own thing.

The only one thing I do ask of Cuddles is for him to be happy and I allow him to just be a horse. I allow him to be himself and do whatever he likes to do. Yes, he's spoilt and yes, he knows it BUT he did point out that although he can be silly, he never does anything dramatic and looks after me. He pointed out that actually he is the one that if others horses need a lead through, say past a large lorry for example, he puts his sensible head on and leads them past! So true, and I do know that he knows where to draw the line. I know him so well and, to be honest, I don't worry what others think.

My boy has the life he chooses, and his very cheeky and funny character shows he's an extremely happy horse, I very rarely have to tell him off for being naughty – why would he be naughty when he has the life he wants? We have a bond and a two-way understanding. I have had many vets tell me that he is a very a lucky horse, but I'm the lucky one and I'm so thankful to have him in my life. He is no longer the scrawny horse he was over three years ago; his condition couldn't be better. Well maybe if he lost a little weight but, as he admitted to Jackie, food is high on his priority list! He has gone from 14.1hh, from the age of six when I first bought him, to 15hh before he was eight, which is late for horse growth, but he simply blossomed with love and proper care. He rarely windsucks nowadays, only when he has to see the vet, or meets new people and feels nervous. His transformation is all through love and allowing him to be the happy horse he wants to be. Jackie picked up on his happiness and contentment; that is so wonderful to hear. I was also delighted when Cuddles mentioned about our special horse portrait. This was amazing to hear but was even more so as he thought we would be repeating it! We are, this summer! He even suggested that I should put a daisy chain in my hair as that would look so sweet. Bless him, and for him, I will do that and actually, with my long dark hair I think it would be very artistic and sweet indeed.

My reading with Jackie has made me understand my boy even more and love him more than I did before, which I didn't think was possible! After my reading I went straight to see him and I could tell in his eyes he knew what had just happened, he literally gave me a kiss, which has never happened! It is usually me kissing him and then him giving me a bunt as if to say, 'Enough thanks, now get off!'

I can't thank Jackie enough for how she has touched my life; she is truly gifted and amazing. I truly appreciate that every day is precious with Cuddles and not just for his love and fun, but in memory of my mum as the amazing connection that I feel with my boy, and my love of horses, was all started by her.

*****

True intuition from her 'Mum'...

Linda and her dog Saffi

I have always had an affinity with dogs and have had one constantly in my life for the past thirty years.

I had a black Labrador called Ellie who I got from Sarah, a lady I often saw when out walking. About five years ago, when Ellie was eight years old, I had the opportunity of getting another one from Sarah. She told me she was breeding from one of her black Labradors, but I told her that the timing wasn't right because there were other things going on in my life. I have to admit, it pained me to say that! Once the puppies were born I resisted going over to see them for a few weeks but, in the end, I had to go. When I got there Sarah said all the black females were sold and there was just one yellow female left, she was actually the only yellow in the litter. I sighed and said I didn't want a yellow one and left feeling rather relieved, as I wasn't supposed to be having another one anyway.

After my visit, in my mind's eye, I kept seeing this image of a yellow lab streaking through some woods and it just would not go away. In the end I called Sarah and said I would have her but by this time the pup had been booked for viewing. There were actually two other interested parties but Sarah added me to the list just in case. I was somewhat taken aback as I had thought this was beginning to feel as if it was meant to be.

A few days later Sarah told me one of the parties had pulled out and the other one was not sure. I was going on holiday to France and Sarah said she would definitely know by the time I came back. By this time I was feeling confident the pup would be mine, but when I came back I was told that the other party definitely wanted her. I put the phone down and cried and said to my partner that she was meant to be mine – I could not believe this was happening, as I could not stop seeing her with me in my mind's eye.

Roll on another week and I got another phone call to say... the pup was mine as the other people had pulled out also! I was over the moon and shortly afterwards went to pick up Saffi as I had decided to name her. At that time, Saffi looked like the classic Andrex puppy as she was the biggest in the litter and quite plump and luscious. Six months later she looked quite different, more like a hound, and looking fit and lean. She was very fast and would tear through the woods like streak lightening – just as I had always seen her in my mind's eye, which was quite amazing!!

She loved to leap into the river or chase through the gorse on the moor without giving her safety a second thought. She was crazy and so happy. She loved throwing her body around, and chasing balls was her idea of heaven. I started to do agility training with her and she loved it – she was very focused and fast for a Labrador and extremely willing to work.

She got on very well with Ellie and they would often play fight together. Ellie would be making a lot of growling noises and Saffi, goading her on, but with lots of tail wagging. Saffi would often do this from under the coffee table so that Ellie couldn't get to her!

As Ellie was getting older, and when we were out on walks, Saffi was always checking to see where she was and wouldn't go on without her.

Sadly Ellie died at the age of thirteen. She was such a heart-felt, friendly, loving dog; it was hard to see her go. Saffi was also lost without her and, when we were out for walks, she was constantly looking back for Ellie.

After a couple of weeks after Ellie died, I decided to take Saffi to a physiotherapist to be checked out. I was a bit concerned, as she limped sometimes after a particularly energetic walk, and I wanted to make sure that agility was the right thing for her, as she is a Labrador; maybe we should be trying other things. I was also wondering whether there were some things I could do to help with the limp and the back leg that seemed stiff sometimes when I dried her off after a walk.

The physio gave her a thorough examination and she said that Saffi seemed to be in a lot of pain and there seemed to be something very wrong with her. I have to say, I was rather taken aback, but she suggested that I get her X-rayed so that she would know what we were dealing with. She also said she should immediately be given painkillers to calm her system down. She said she would contact the vet and tell him what she was suggesting. I was somewhat alarmed, as I had thought this would be a very brief check up and some advice but it seemed to be turning into something a lot bigger. In the next few days I found myself at the vet with Saffi getting painkillers and making an appointment for quite a few X-rays.

The X-rays came back and I was told they were showing a narrowing between two vertebrae on her lower back. There was also a problem with her shoulder joint – there seemed to be calcification and bony growth. The vet said to keep her on painkillers and then bring her back. I took her back and the vet re-examined her (this included Saffi being held very tight and much to her obvious dislike) and the vet said she still felt the same so referred me on to an orthopaedic consultant.

By this time I was getting very anxious – I had not long lost one of my dogs and now there seemed to be serious problems with this one and she wasn't even five-years-old!

I had been thinking about speaking to an animal communicator for Saffi anyway because I wanted to know a bit more about what was going on in her mind; she is a very sensitive dog and I love the idea of communicating more closely with her, it is something that I have always been fascinated about. I looked on the Internet and saw Jackie's name and I had an immediate gut reaction to contact her. It happened very easily, I emailed her and a time to speak on the phone was set up. Strangely enough the time for the appointment of the consultant had come up and it was on the same Friday. I had Jackie down for 12.00 noon and then the consultant at 6.00 pm.

Jackie called me and I immediately felt she was right for Saffi and me. I appreciated her sense of humour and there was a lightness around her. I didn't say anything about Saffi but Jackie just started to talk with her and told me things. She told me that Saffi wasn't an, 'in your face sort of dog' and she had a 'bendy back'. So true! When Saffi comes up to say hello, her back seems to curve as she is wagging her tail so hard. She mentioned other things that Saffi was showing her and one of them was that my other dog was in the garden... yes Ellie's ashes were in the garden! At this point I still had said nothing at all about Saffi and the fears I had around her.

Jackie then said that, according to Saffi, her mobility was fine but then she was seeing a picture of Saffi putting out her foreleg and pulling it back. Jackie said it seems like she is saying she doesn't want to be checked. Jackie said, 'This may sound a bit strange or bold… but Saffi says she doesn't have any growths?!" Jackie said she didn't know what was going on with such a young dog, and importantly that she didn't diagnose, but Saffi is saying, "I am not in pain." She backed this up saying that she was not crying out etc. which was the case. I was so relieved to hear this (my gut instinct was that she was not suffering awful pain in spite of what the vets had said – we do know our own animals and their individual behaviours) and I explained to Jackie that I had been told Saffi had problems but that I was really unsure about the whole thing. Saffi then made us both laugh by saying, "Please stop crying Mother!"

Jackie said that, according to Saffi, she has strained her left shoulder but she walks fine – she is a bit of a 'shoulder dog'. (She is one that tends to weight bear to her shoulders.) Saffi then showed Jackie her spine and said, "It is fine and straight. There is just one slight problem, which puts everything slightly out, but please don't overreact and I am not in pain." Jackie told me Saffi is now showing the base of her back and saying I won't hurt her if I touch her there. I agreed it didn't, and Saffi asked me just to scratch her there as she loved it. That was incredible to me, as I had thought that when she turned her back end to me she was telling me that she was in pain, but actually she just wanted me to scratch her there. Now I do it all the time and she LOVES it!

At this point I told Jackie what had been going on with Saffi. I explained that she was going to see a specialist later that same day and I was taking her X-rays for a second opinion too. Jackie then said that Saffi really made her feel (although she said she could be wrong) that she did not have joint degeneration and she doesn't want to be checked anymore. Jackie said that she was going to talk to Saffi and tell her, like you would a child; that it is for her own good and this is happening to make sure all is okay... but Saffi was still saying to Jackie that there wasn't much wrong! Jackie said she could only go on the info that Saffi was giving her and hoped to goodness that this really was the case.

She then told Jackie how she loves going away with me, and loves us doing things together. She is very happy and loves her life! We also touched on hydrotherapy and I know it made such a huge difference for my lovely Ellie that it may be beneficial to Saffi too. I thanked Jackie for her insight and said I would let her know of the outcome.

I was surprised and delighted with this interaction and also much more relaxed about the imminent appointment with the specialist. I was also amazed at how different Saffi appeared to be after the session – she seemed to be lighter and more relaxed. I drove that evening with Saffi to see him, and I immediately warmed to him and so did Saffi. He gave her a thorough examination, which she allowed in a more relaxed fashion. Usually she tenses up her body so the vet finds it difficult to feel what is going on.

He then showed me the X-rays and said there was some wear and tear and told me he felt that, yes, her walking was a little bit off, but that was nothing to worry about and there was nothing to be done! He said she did have quite prominent shoulders, but that was just how she was made. I asked if physiotherapy would be good for her but he didn't seem to think so as she did not need it. He also said she didn't seem to be in pain and there was no need for any more painkillers. That was a relief, as I think they were upsetting her stomach and Jackie had mentioned this too.

He did agree that maybe her body may have had tension after Ellie had died. It could have been tight and have brought on discomfort in her back. He beamed and said how wonderful it was to finish his week on such a happy note as it was unusual to be saying all is okay! I drove home smiling to myself when I realised that there was no big operation looming and goodness knows what else.

I just had to get back to tell Jackie the outcome and just how accurate the information was… What Saffi was saying *was* true, and also to thank her for giving Saffi a chance to tell her side of the story. The relief has been immense.

*****

More than just a rabbit and so loved…

Mark and his rabbit Bailey

Bailey came into my life in October 2012. At the time I was working as a manager for a garden centre that also had a large pet and aquatic department. Although I was not looking for a new pet at the time, I would always go and have a look at the new animals that had just come in.

One day I noticed we had a new, and rather unusual, rabbit who had come in. He was beautiful, all black with big ears and the size of a cat, even though he was only six months old! I was informed that he was a continental giant breed. As I approached the glass, he excitedly bounded over towards me. I knew from that very moment that I wanted him and quickly asked one of the girls to reserve him for me. Due to his size he would need to be kept as a house rabbit as there were no rabbit cages large enough to house him. I decided that I would keep him in my bedroom at home and give him a dog cage and bed to sleep in. This would be larger and also suitable for his toilet area too, and fortunately he was already fully litter tray trained. I remember afterwards thinking about how I was going to break this news to my parents! Gently!

When I brought him home, he quickly settled in and amazed me with his wonderful and very loving personality. He was adored by everybody and acted more like a dog than a rabbit; it was quite amazing really. I saw personality changes as he grew slightly older and calmed down; he was such a laid back and chilled out rabbit. As a youngster he would have mad periods, racing round and round my room, and I especially recall one occasion where he managed to jump up onto my computer desk sending everything flying! As he calmed down he was simply no trouble at all and we gave him the free run of my room and the upstairs landing area in my house. He was so happy there and preferred to sit down and watch the world go by and, very occasionally, his natural rabbit tendencies to nibble something came back: wallpaper, carpet or the odd book left in his path!

We had a little routine where every night he would know what time I was coming up to bed and he would wait for me. Whilst I was getting ready, I would give him a rabbit biscuit and then he would wait for me to call him. When I said his name, he came racing towards me for a cuddle and some love before bedtime. He was so adorable; while I stroked him, he would kick his legs in the air and grind his teeth softly like a purr. As the years went by our connection seemed to just get stronger and I loved him to bits.

The vets that looked after him his whole life were wonderful to him – he was quite the star when he would go for his nails to be cut or injections. They all loved him, and he knew it!

One morning in early November 2015 I noticed that Bailey had a very sore looking eye and as he had been a little off his food for a few days, I immediately took him to the vets. They thought he may have scratched his eye and treated him with antibiotics and eye drops. As the days went by Bailey was not getting better and still refused to eat much. I took him back to the vets who started treating him for a nasty parasite called E.Cuniculi which can have devastating effects if not treated. They also suggested that maybe he had toothache and this was why he was reluctant to eat. A blood test confirmed the worst; it was E.Cuniculi. We had to take him back to the vets every day for a month for his medication. There was no cure from this parasite, but we hoped that the medications would stop him from becoming even sicker.

As the weeks went by, we saw him, and his personality change. He lost such a lot of weight, became depressed, and did not want to move around as much as before. The most devastating symptom of this illness was that he developed nerve damage in his face which stopped him from eating by his own means so we had to constantly hand-feed him food. Towards the final weeks he developed nerve damage in one of his back legs which began to take his mobility away. I knew that because I loved him so much I could not let him suffer like this and sadly, on the 24th December 2015, I drove him to the vets. We had a long talk about the options, and the vet and I agreed that there was nothing more that could be done for him. He went to sleep in my arms at 4.30pm.

The days, weeks and months after were really hard and even now, as I write this, I just miss him so much. It was around early March when I contacted Jackie for a spirit animal reading, having found her website on the Internet. Jackie made an appointment for our telephone conversation and we had the most amazing time.

Initially she described Bailey's personality and it was just so accurate. We always said that Bailey was more like a dog than a rabbit, and this was one of the first things that Jackie told me! Bailey's condition developed some very specific symptoms and I listened, quite amazed, while Jackie described them to me. Bailey was telling her how the vets kept looking in his mouth while it was his kidneys that were the problem! Bailey told me that there was nothing more that I could have done. He wanted to thank me, and my parents, for the daily trips to the vets over several months! In the later stages of the illness, Bailey was hand fed with salads, dandelion leaves and carrot tops, as he was unable to eat by himself. Jackie also described this to me and again he wanted to express his gratitude.

At home, we have a second rabbit downstairs called Phoebe. She is my mum's rabbit and the two had never met. Well, you can image my amazement when Jackie told me that Bailey knew she was downstairs, he described her as a grey hairy type (which she is!) and even gave me her nickname 'Princess', which is what I call her. Now knowing that I lived at home with my parents, Jackie seemed a little confused and asked if I was moving, and why another house seemed to be brought to her attention. The reason for this was that I was having the call, not from my own house, but my girlfriend's house who, incidentally, also has a rabbit. Bailey then took the opportunity to tell us that my girlfriends rabbit was not like him – yes, she is the complete opposite; a pure white one!

Bailey talked about my bedroom to Jackie, even showing her the flickering lights that used to irritate me when they did it, let alone him. I was just so touched when Jackie talked about me keeping some of Bailey's fur I had saved from his brush and keep in a drawer in my room. He told her how he missed being physically with me and thought about me so often, and knew that I did the same about him. We both laughed at Bailey showing his love of cardboard toilet rolls to Jackie (they were his favourite) and his love of running into rooms that he should not have been in. His fantastic personality just shone through.

Jackie, thank you so much, you have an amazing gift that you use to help people through their grief. I felt so much happier after the conversation knowing that the powerful connection that Bailey and I had in life, is still there. Even though I cannot turn the clock back, he is still with me always and in my heart forever. Finally I asked Jackie if she thought I would see Bailey again one day, to which she replied, 'Yes, most definitely." The whole experience was just amazing and one that I will never forget.

*****

A wonderful and trustworthy family girl...

Nichola and her dog Shakira

My name is Nichola and I live with my husband and two young children and I have always grown up with dogs. Over ten years ago, whilst on a weekend break, my now-husband and I met and fell in love with a little malamute puppy. We brought her home with us there and then and from that moment, she became very much one of the family. She was a pure white, tiny ball of fur who we named Shakira. Very quickly she became my fur baby! She came everywhere with us, and all of our extended family also treated her like one of the family. She grew into a very big dog, but was the most affectionate and loving animal you could ever meet, and also the smartest dog I have ever known. My Grandad would tell people about her all the time and he always said she could do everything but speak to you!

Shakira and I have always had a close bond and she had her own ways of letting us know what she wanted. For example: she would rap the letterbox when she was ready for a walk, jingle the keys in the back door if she wanted to go outside and she would paw the washing machine if she wanted her water bowl filled up! I knew her like the back of my hand, so when I realised that she just wasn't herself one evening I really was worried sick. She had been in the kitchen with me and I could tell there was something different about her breathing – she just seemed more tired than normal so I contacted our vet. She had various tests done throughout the next two days, but to no conclusion and she was still deteriorating. On the Friday she ended up staying the night at the vets for observation and further testing.

This made me even more worried as I could not be with her to comfort her – she had only ever spent one night away from family since she came into our lives. The next morning I received the devastating phone call from our vet to tell me that Shakira had passed away during the night. I was truly heartbroken losing her, but what made it even worse was that I had not been with her, I had not been able to say goodbye, and had so many unanswered questions.

In the weeks following her passing I was really struggling with her loss and was tormenting myself with all the unanswered questions. This was when I began looking into how I could get the answers I needed. I have always believed that animals could communicate with us and that they have spirits too, so I started searching on the Internet to try to find an animal psychic / medium who could help me. When I discovered Jackie's website, and read about the spirit animal readings and the testimonials, I wasted no time in contacting her to arrange a reading.

When Jackie contacted me for my reading I cried and I laughed at the conversation with Shakira. Firstly Jackie was able to let me know that Shakira was okay now but that it had taken her a while to settle in the spirit world, as it all happened so unexpectedly she had not been prepared or ready to leave us just yet. While it broke my heart to hear this, it was also nice to know that she loved us as much as we loved her and that she didn't want to leave us. She was also able to let me know that she was not in pain and that she just went to sleep. I asked if I had missed any signs that she was ill, but she told Jackie that I knew her like the back of my hand and couldn't have done anything else. This was so comforting to know that Shakira had felt the bond that I always knew we had.

She did make me laugh though, as she told Jackie about the cat that walks around the vets practice and how it kept her amused while she was there – it really is a cheeky cat and always taunted her any time we were there! The morning I received the devastating phone call I had had a really uneasy feeling from the moment I got up. During the reading Shakira told Jackie that she knew that subconsciously I knew that she had passed before I got the call – we really did know each other inside out. She also said how I was always adamant that she could understand everything I said to her, and she confirmed that she really did! She was very persistent and would never give up until she got what she wanted. It was good to know that she hadn't lost that trait, as during the reading she showed Jackie a grey husky with piercing blue eyes, not once but four times! So far I haven't been able to understand the significance of this dog, but if Shakira was that adamant over that image I have no doubt that I will piece it together some day.

My son is still very young and Shakira actually told Jackie that he was chirping away about her all the time – he does, every day he talks about her still. I told Jackie that he had been asking me when was I going to go and bring Shakira home. Jackie told me to tell him that she couldn't come home but she was watching him from Heaven and just to think of her walking on the clouds. He did laugh when I told him that and said, "But Mummy she is the same colour as the clouds, I won't be able to see her, silly billy." I often worried that since our children came along that Shakira felt left out but Jackie assured me that Shakira didn't see it that way; she said that the kids come first and that she just gained a job and wanted to protect them. This was so true, as she would stay close to them if there were visitors in the house and when they were babies, she would sleep beside the moses basket when they were asleep in it.

Shakira told Jackie that she would lie across the doorway and that I would have to step over her all the time. She did! She also knew that since she passed I hated going into the kitchen as it was a constant reminder that she was not there. So Shakira suggested, to try and help ease my pain, to just step 'over her' whenever I feel like I need to and to smile at the spots where she always lay. I have been doing this every day and it has helped – she always knew when I needed her. She made us laugh when she told Jackie about how she used to lie on the sofa and being such a big dog she would take up the whole three-seater sofa! She also told Jackie about how she would lie on her side and look up at me to get her belly rubbed, and she told her to tell me to remember her that way. That has helped too as she did make me laugh when she did that as I knew exactly what that look was for!

No matter where we walked Shakira, we were always stopped by people admiring her. She actually brought that up in the reading too and said how lots of people would comment that she was a 'smashing dog', and that really is what many people did say. She knew she was a gorgeous girl and told Jackie that she was one-in-a-million and that there would never be another one like her – this is so very true!

At the end of the reading Shakira said that she had a wonderful life and that she was one of the family. This was really good to hear, as she really was regarded as one of the family by everyone; she would come everywhere with us and was my big fur baby whom I trusted whole-heartedly. As I have said to Jackie; I will always have a Shakira shaped hole in my heart but thanks to this reading, I can now focus on all the years of lovely memories we made with her, instead of all the unanswered questions I had prior to contacting Jackie. I really cannot thank Jackie enough.

*****

Saved only to leave too soon...

Beth and her dog Barnaby

Barnaby... Where do you start with Barnaby! Barnaby was found on the streets of Romania with his brother as abandoned pups. Full of worms, underweight and covered in lice, they were left to freeze in -15 degrees temperatures. I fell in love with his picture and reserved him immediately!

We waited three long months until he arrived. When he did he was a skinny, smelly and overgrown six-month-old pup who had no idea what a collar and lead were for! He didn't know what a house was and was terrified of many things.

Throughout my nine months with this gorgeous boy, amazingly he grew and grew until he was huge! He turned into the most loving boy, who loved nothing more than a cuddle on the sofa. He won over my existing dog and they loved to play, and like any puppy, he was into everything he shouldn't have been, and destroyed many possessions! He was beautiful and unique; he turned heads wherever he went. Everybody loved him for the big goof he was!

Unfortunately, pretty soon after I got him, he began to show pain in his rear end after exercise. This slowly worsened to the point that he couldn't manage even a ten-minute walk. X-rays of his hips and spine showed nothing, so he went off to the top specialists in the country. He stayed for a week and, after a huge amount of tests, later showed lots of abnormalities in his bloods, muscles etc. but unfortunately, no real diagnosis. They put him on a drug trial for nerve pain.

He came home and we had many happy times. He managed to walk and play a bit more and generally seemed a much happier boy. Sadly though, three months later, the same symptoms returned, this time with added panting and jaw symptoms. So back he went for another week, but again no conclusions. He came home and was on strict rest with a slow exercise regime. Within three weeks my boy had withdrawn; he was refusing to get out of bed for his dinner (his favourite thing!), he didn't want to play and was extremely distressed. He panted constantly, to the point it looked like he may have a stroke and was kicking at his stomach until it was red raw. Multiple trips to the vets did nothing and on the Saturday he began to hallucinate. At that point I decided enough was enough. He had been through so much, nobody had an answer and he was clearly in huge amounts of pain despite being on maximum pain medication. My boy went to sleep with his head on my lap whilst I told him I loved him and was so glad he came to me. Aged one year and three months old, he left the world that had dealt him the cruellest of hands in so many ways.

I was distraught – not only had my boy gone, but I had no answers and therefore I felt tremendous guilt about whether I had done the right thing? Was there anything else we could have done? Every waking thought was about him and although I thought I might be going mad, I could swear he was trying to contact me and my other dog, who began acting bizarrely at times like she could see him.

I reached out to Jackie to find some answers and to try and get some peace of mind. I really wanted assurance that he knew he was loved and wanted.

Jackie made immediate contact with Barnaby in the form of coughing! This was as she answered the phone to me and she apologised. When it happened again a little later, we recognised this was from him indicating his symptoms of extreme thirst, which led to him coughing. From the moment I got him he was obsessed with water, knowing where it was and also the need to drink! He described himself as being into everything but without a nasty bone in his body, which was him through and through! He also said he loved a cuddle, which he did – I miss cuddling him so much.

Where no vets had been able to find an answer, Jackie received one from Barnaby himself! He mentioned various symptoms and said that he had had an 'adverse reaction' to something. Jackie said that she had heard a word, which had thrown her, but if okay, she would say it any way. She said, "Rabies," which Jackie quite rightly thought was odd having assumed he was British. When I revealed he wasn't, it all became clear. Barnaby was putting across that he had a rare reaction to his rabies vaccination. This caused his system to break down in different places each time, which was so accurate to his illness! Jackie admitted that earlier on in the reading, that he had said it was like he was 'mashed', but she had no idea what it meant so she didn't pass it on. Once he had got us to understand why this was, he repeated that, by the end, his insides felt like 'mash'. He also gave Jackie a tucked up feeling in her tummy, which explains why he was kicking himself there at the end! My poor, poor boy. Jackie said that after the call she would look up on the Internet and see what she could find out about his symptoms. I said I would do the same.

Jackie repeated from Barnaby, "Thank you – you did a good thing and had I not come to you, I would have probably died on the concrete." It was then I told Jackie that he had been rescued from the street nearly frozen to the ground. Although bittersweet, as he wouldn't have had that fateful injection if he hadn't been coming to me, he most certainly would have met an awful end in Romania. He mentioned Brittany in France which, I believe, is his memory of his crossing to the UK but he was very clear he remembers his life as being with me, not his previous one abroad.

Earlier on Jackie said she could tell that he knew he was spoilt and didn't always listen! She got the impression his recall wasn't good – very true, he would often reluctantly wait for me but rarely came back!

He called himself 'alluring' which is such an accurate a word for him! People would literally come out of their houses to stroke him, as he was such a beautiful and unusual dog. He also called himself 'a valuable stray' which I think is his way of justifying his value to me as priceless.

True to form, and wanting to be centre of attention, he also wished that he could have fairy lights around his picture on the wall so he could be a 'star'!!!! This is a picture we have had done since his death and gave me comfort he knew he was there. Of course his wishes will be honoured.

More than anything, Jackie could assure me he knew he was loved and that we really did try everything to save him. His words were 'you had no choice' in that final day which gave me the closure I needed to have done the right thing.

I also wanted to know if my other dog could see him and he said, he was 'budging her up on the sofa' which was so typical of his behaviour. She's a tiny dog and he was huge and he literally would push her, and anyone else in his way, off the sofa to get the best seat!

I think the most poignant moment for me was that Barnaby showed Jackie a cloud that I thought might be him. Jackie asked if I had seen such a thing and indeed, a few days after his death, whilst on my own in the garden, I saw a cloud and was certain it looked like him. I tried to take a picture but it moved, but it had his unique ears and he looked like he was running across the sky. During the reading Barnaby told Jackie it *was* him showing himself to me and was so glad that I had seen it. I had told nobody of the cloud and that was true affirmation that Barnaby was still with me. Another emotional moment was Barnaby telling Jackie he had seen a German Shepherd in spirit the day he died as he went. My previous dog from my childhood was put to sleep at that vets and she was a German Shepherd. Jackie picked up on the fact it was her back legs that caused her passing and it gave me great comfort to know she had been there for him. Barnaby's words were, "I simply went to sleep." I am so glad he did not feel any pain.

Shockingly though, Barnaby also revealed he did not want me to adopt again from Romania. Although his case was so rare, he felt there were other diseases and he couldn't bear to see me go through 'hell' (his own words) again. He felt that my next dog would be a runt and my current dog (who was also a runt!) would look after it. I have to say though, she's the least mothering type of dog and so if he's right it will be a miracle! The revelation regarding Romania really surprised me as I felt he would want me to help again, but he was adamant! Once again he did say 'thank you' and told me I did a good thing in taking him. It is something I will never ever regret.

Barnaby also wanted me to let the vets know of my findings. I said I would, Jackie suggested it might be best to say simply that I that I had been talking to somebody (well, I had!) and researched Google (which I did!) and the symptoms so clearly fitted. I emailed them the same day as the reading and, should another dog show such symptoms, at least his information might prove invaluable. They too might not be able to be saved, but at least the vets would have a better understanding of what they were dealing with and treat accordingly.

I will continue to miss Barnaby every day but I am comforted to know he's still with me in spirit. More than anything I have been able to let go of the guilt and unanswered questions surrounding his passing and begin to move on. I can't wait to see you on the other side my handsome lad, we've got time to make up for!

*****

A dog who truly was the greatest gift...

Tracy and her dog Hogan

I first met Hogan when he was just six weeks old. I love all dogs, and always have – but had a special affinity for the rough collie, ever since I had watched Lassie as a small child! The time was right to bring a dog into the family, to join my children Alex (then eleven) and Freya (just three, and still a baby herself). At just six weeks, Hogan was still too young to come home with us, but we travelled to observe the litter with their mother and make a choice. I worried that I would never be able to do that, and would want to take them all home! I need not have worried at all, all eight bundles of fluff were let loose in the living room, licking furiously; stumpy tails wagging, but after a while wandered off to play with each other. All except one pup. He climbed onto my son's lap, getting as close as he could, and looked up as if to say, 'I'm your dog. You don't need to choose, for I choose you.' He stayed there for the duration of the visit, and thus the decision was made by Hogan himself!

All eight puppies were given names at a puppy naming party that the breeder had organised with her family. It was a sweet thing to do, although she knew that most of the puppies would be given names chosen by their new families. We had several names in mind; however, Hogan just looked like he should remain as Hogan, and so it was.

Hogan was our self-appointed protector from the day he came into our lives. He was such a gentleman, never playing rough with girls, as though he knew they needed careful handling! He was such a respectful dog, never snapping at anyone, even when young hands ventured where they shouldn't. On walks, he would run and bounce vertically, as if on springs, the only part of him visible amongst all the corn were his ears as he bobbed up and down! He never ventured too far, though – always turning back to make sure I was okay, and circling me at wide range as though I was part of a flock he had to look after! He had many endearing habits and traits, including the one where he would know exactly when he was to be fed and would not let me deviate from it! He would push his nose into my lap when it was time, and if I didn't get up right away he would back off a few steps and stamp his feet – literally!

When Hogan was a young boy of around three or four, I went through some very dark times personally. There were times when I felt he was my only friend. I lost count of the number of times I sobbed into his thick fur, where he would press himself into me as close as he could, gazing up at me and silently agreeing with every word I said – be it right or wrong. The loyalty and love he gave me were beyond measure, and without bounds. This is where some people just don't understand, people can, on occasion, let you down and be less than kind. A dog will never, ever do this – and will always return your love and care a million times over. Their spirits are infinitely pure, and as a result end up teaching you a good deal more than you could ever teach them!

Eventually I remarried, and although reluctant to get attached to a dog after losing his own some years before, my husband grew to love Hogan – as everyone always did! Hogan was impossible to keep out of your heart.

Hogan was a healthy boy, not needing much veterinary attention until he was nine and needed surgery for a benign tumour on his unmentionables. He recovered well, but just being without him for a day was awful. We had an excellent vet, but Hogan never liked leaving his family and disliked going, so when he became very ill at ten and a half and had to spend time in a specialist dog hospital to try and find out what was wrong, it was truly awful. I felt as though I was betraying him, leaving him there and his not understanding why. I remember coming home and praying as I had never prayed in my life, for spirit not to take my dog and begging for more time. Hogan fought hard to stay, and I fought to keep him, and after a few weeks he rallied round. I nursed him, as he had nursed me, and we became even closer.

In his latter years, Hogan developed arthritis and would collapse without warning, his back legs letting him down. No medication suited him, and no matter what we tried the drugs would make him violently sick. We did, however, find a herbal combination that helped a great deal in his later years. He could no longer go for walks, instead choosing to potter round our fairly large garden – still verbally warning any cat, bird or any other intruder to stay off his territory. He also developed deafness, and could only tell if someone came to the door by smell. He slept most of the day, during his thirteenth year, waking only to eat. Still he soldiered on, never complaining, and remaining the loving boy he always was.

The night before he passed to spirit had been as normal. In the morning, my husband found him in the kitchen, a place he never went as he disliked the floor. He did not seem right, and Paul lifted him into the living room where he collapsed onto his side. He never got up again, although he tried twice before giving up. I called the vet in panic, and my daughter and I lay with him, waiting for them to arrive. It never occurred to me that we would lose him that day. As I lay with him stroking his head, I saw something which I now know I was privileged to see, and Hogan's last loving gift to me. It is hard for me to explain it in words, but I will attempt to. As I gazed into his eyes, I saw Hogan - his spirit, his personality, the very 'essence' of him, separate from his physical self. It was far from just seeing the biological function fade, and more of a separation between the spiritual and physical. I saw my beautiful boy rise up and leave, and I knew he had chosen to go and that I had witnessed it. The vet arrived and did tests, which we actually made them do twice. The vets told us that there was nothing we could do and we had to let him go. It was the hardest thing I have ever done in my life, because his heart was still beating and I was desperately hoping for a miracle. I knew deep down in my soul that my beautiful boy had gone before the vet got anywhere near him. Once again, it was Hogan's decision, Hogan's choice, and no-one else's. As always.

No matter how many people told me that, at almost 14 years old, Hogan had lived a long life; it provided no comfort. You are just never ready to lose someone you love so much. Logically, I suppose it was true, but emotionally it made no sense at all. I felt as though someone had torn into my very soul, I can honestly say that I have never known pain like it. I did have support as the family was totally heartbroken, and I was not alone, but at the same time the agony was a very isolating thing. I just wanted my dog back, and couldn't think of anything else. This is what led me to Jackie, a small ray of hope blinking in what was a terrible darkness for me.

In the days after losing Hogan, I was sat at my computer in the corner of the room. I was desperately searching for comfort from others who had lost their beloved pets, and trying to find evidence of survival of the spirit. This was how I found Jackie, whose name stood out, and I felt that it was the right thing to do to contact her. There were others listed, but I somehow felt guided to choose her. I had felt so miserable since Hogan has passed; I could not 'feel' him around and had only emptiness and pain.

My husband asked me what I wanted for Christmas, and I told him that if I couldn't have my baby back I wanted an appointment to speak to him again. It was arranged and I clung on to the date I was given and looked forward to it far more than anything I had ever anticipated.

Jackie was down to earth, caring and lovely. I sat with my daughter as we chatted with her and Hogan over Skype and I was completely amazed. Nothing she said was generic in nature, and there was no doubt in our minds that it was our lovely boy she was talking to! She mentioned that Hogan never went up the stairs, which he didn't, not even when he was young, except on firework night! She told us that he could jump vertically (a special trait of the young Hogan) and demonstrated this perfectly. What was truly amazing is that she said that someone had been 'writing or completing something' to do with Hogan, which was really astounding. My daughter had started an art and written project all about Hogan as part of a college assessment, which was difficult for her to complete as she was only halfway through it when he passed. Hogan told us it was A+, and we were amazed as she did indeed get a distinction for her work only days before. He also told Jackie that university was on its way, (for Freya) and mentioned

Bournemouth which was unreal, as Freya had been applying to universities around the country, and Bournemouth was a consideration at the time. Hogan said that he was 'everyone's friend', which he undeniably was. Any visitor had to make a fuss of him first, before he would let them sit down and chat! He reminded us that he had 'a clock in his head' and knew when he would be fed, which was so true, it made me tear up remembering it. He mentioned my own Dad, with whom Hogan had a very special relationship. He also spoke of a memorial, a red rose tree, which I had already planned on planting in the spring. There are no other red flowers in the garden, but we decided on red to symbolise love and it was so lovely to know that he approved of my plan. He said that he had had a 'full length life' and hadn't had a single worry in it, apart from disliking his nails being cut, which again was so accurate. He told us that at the end he 'had had enough' which was a comfort in as much, as that it confirmed my belief that Hogan chose to go to spirit. Jackie described his back legs and how they would buckle, and the weak spot on his back that would make his legs give out if it was touched.

So much information was given during the time we had, including the fact that he was now 'seated with many people'. This made perfect sense, as Hogan was so much more of a people dog than anything else, and was exactly as Jackie described him. He also told us that he could 'play with the television' if he wanted to, which is exactly what happened the very next day! Once I acknowledged him out loud, the television worked again and hasn't been a problem since. He even mentioned the 'annoying Christmas lights' that were flashing into our living room from a house across the street! He also confirmed that I had indeed heard his heavy paws plodding around the living room whilst I was upstairs, which was so reassuring to know that it was not my imagination. Hogan even knew I had found Jackie whilst sitting in a far corner of the room on my computer, and that my husband had glimpsed him, just for a second. I believe he had a significant role to play in finding Jackie. So many deeply personal things were relayed to us during our time on Skype, that after it was over, I cried with sheer relief. My daughter drew a great deal of comfort from Hogan's own words: that he would remain her protector for always.

The spirit communication has taught me many things. Life does indeed go on, our beloved animals do survive this 'change' and they continue to love us until we can all be together again. Being able to talk to my beloved boy through Jackie has soothed my aching heart and made his passing just that little bit easier to bear. I know now that this separation is only temporary, and that no loving dog ever truly leaves the person(s) who love them. I am eternally grateful to Jackie for the comfort she gave to me and my family, and to Hogan, who in his own words said, "I was blessed, and so were they!"

*****

Postscript

Once again a huge thank you to friends, Joy, Shirley, Diane, Becci, Nicky, Iona, Yvon and Penny as my pre-checkers and post-checkers – your help is very much appreciated.

To my guides Rolf and Stan, without you my life would not be what it is. To my darling Sally who helps me teach so many people and loves to work with me, as I do her. Last but definitely not least, a huge thanks to each every one of you who trusted me to communicate with your animal and wrote your story for this book. I know I have touched your lives but believe me, you and your animals have touched mine.

Thank you for choosing and reading my book and if you like what I do and want to read more, here are the other books that I have done too.

They are all available on Amazon in paperback and digital. If you don't mind me asking… but if you can spare a minute to write a review about this book (or other ones of mine that you have read) I would be most grateful. It is the public's opinion that helps others make their choice of reading material. So, if you feel this book would be informative, enjoyable or even enlightening to someone else, a few words would help guide them.

If I have worked for you and you think people would like to read your story, then feel free to email me on info@animalpsychic.co.uk and we can go from there. Please don't worry if you have not written a story before, I hadn't until my first book! I can give you a bit of guidance and, as long as you write the gist of it, I can do the rest.

Bless you all and may you and your animals stay well and safe and do enjoy talking to them knowing that they do understand what you say!

If you want to be kept informed of what I am getting up to, TV appearances, what my next book is etc. I do send out the occasional newsletter. If you go on to my website and scroll down to the bottom of the first page, you will see a picture of my cat Buddy, looking very studious and you can sign up from there. I promise, your email address is totally protected and never shared.

Jackie Weaver
'The Animal Psychic'
www.animalpsychic.co.uk